Homesick

Homesick

*Race and Exclusion
in Rural New England*

Emily Walton

Stanford University Press
Stanford, California

Stanford University Press
Stanford, California

Library of Congress Cataloging-in-Publication Data
Names: Walton, Emily C. author
Title: Homesick : race and exclusion in rural New England / Emily Walton.
Description: Stanford, California : Stanford University Press, [2026] | Includes
    bibliographical references and index.
Identifiers: LCCN 2025006110 (print) | LCCN 2025006111 (ebook) |
    ISBN 9781503643932 cloth | ISBN 9781503644519 paperback | ISBN 9781503644526
    ebook
Subjects: LCSH: Minorities—New England—Social conditions | Racism—New
    England | New England—Race relations | New England—Rural conditions
Classification: LCC F15.A1 W35 2026 (print) | LCC F15.A1 (ebook) |
    DDC 305.800974—dc23/eng/20250606

LC record available at https://lccn.loc.gov/2025006110
LC ebook record available at https://lccn.loc.gov/2025006111

Cover design: Ann Weinstock
Cover art: Adobe Stock

The authorized representative in the EU for product safety and compliance is: Mare
Nostrum Group B.V. | Mauritskade 21D | 1091 GC Amsterdam | The Netherlands
| Email address: gpsr@mare-nostrum.co.uk | KVK chamber of commerce
number: 96249943

Contents

Acknowledgments

I would like to express my sincere gratitude to the many generous people who played a part in this book. Most importantly, I am indebted to all the Upper Valley residents who honestly and openly shared their stories for this research. You gave the most precious gift: yourselves. I hope I have represented your perspectives with the respect and care you deserve.

This project would not have been possible without financial support from the Nelson A. Rockefeller Center for Public Policy and the Social Sciences, which provided funding for a faculty research grant and a book manuscript workshop. I am grateful to Richard Wright, Jason Houle, Elizabeth Carpenter-Song, Sarah Mayorga, and Leah Schmalzbauer for contributing their time and expertise to a book manuscript workshop and thank them for their close reading and critical suggestions for revision. I also wish to acknowledge *Rural Sociology* for granting permission to incorporate some of my previously published insights into this work.

I could not have completed this project without the assistance of several Dartmouth undergraduates who served as interviewers and research partners over the years; I offer thanks to Isaiah Miller, Roesha Andre, Kate Wood, Liz Choi, Samantha Hussey, Nashe Mutenda, Gustavo De Almeida Silva, Emma Rodriguez, Uyen Dang, Lily Ren, and Ruba Iqbal. I also wish to thank the students who have written stories for this book's sister project, Humans of the Upper Valley: Lily Ren, Rachel Zhang, Katherine Takoudes, Lauren Hwang, Daniel Lin, Matt Gannon, Kayleigh Bowler, Jessica Brantez, Christian Beck, Paget Chung, Elizabeth Ray, Arshi Mahajan, Gaia Yun, Lauren Groulx, Carrina Chen, Mihir Sardesai, Abenezer Sheberu, and Manu Onteeru. Your efforts have helped bring recognition to so many incredible people in this community.

I am also grateful to the many colleagues who have read and helped me talk through bits and pieces of this project over the years. To my longest-standing colleague, Jason Houle, I appreciate your open door and understand that a document full of tracked changes is how you express your love; I would not be the scholar I am without you. To my friend, colleague, and confidant Janice McCabe, thank you for sharing your wisdom and experience. You are model of integrity, and I so admire the person that you are. Kathryn Lively, I know that I am your favorite. Thanks for always making me laugh and keeping me on my toes. Thank you, Kim Rogers, for sharing your unending cache of ideas and new directions. Greg Sharp, I always feel so validated when we talk. To my savvy and wise mentor in the Department of Geography, Richard Wright, I appreciate your intellectual curiosity. Jonathan Chipman, your expertise has been integral to my success on this and many other projects. Laura McDaniel, you help keep me grounded. Kim Hanchett, you make me smile every day. To all the postdocs and faculty fellows in the Society of Fellows, you are my fountain of youth! I also appreciate Amy Mulligan and Braxton Soderman, the beautiful people in our online group who have cheered me on and helped me stop "faffing about" every day.

I would not be anywhere in this academic life without several significant mentors. My first and best mentor, David Takeuchi, is the most intelligent, humble, and generous person I know. Thank you for inviting me into the room. I believe in me because you believe in me. To the other members of the Dream Team (aka The Executive Committee), Jerry Herting and Stew Tolnay, thank you for keeping David in line. But seriously, thank you, Stew, for pushing me on the classic questions. And Jerry, I appreciate your easy laugh and how you model balance. Your secrets to survivin' got me on a train bound for somewhere. Steph Robert, you are a goddess. I am fortunate to be among the thousands you count as mentees and friends.

To my developmental editor, Jeanne Barker-Nunn, you are *everything*. You saved this project from the dustbin on more than one occasion, and your gentle guidance has made the final product more than I could have imagined.

Thank you to my family for bringing the love. To all my parents—Betsie, Bill, Consuelo, Lynn, and Raz—I appreciate that you have been genuinely interested. Thank you to my sister, Kymber, for being the best listener. Camille and Josie, I am grateful for your patience and unconditional support over the last few years of my obsession with turning this "book" into a book. Joel, you are my number one. *Estamos juntos*.

Introduction

I came for the job. In 2012, my family and I moved from our urban home on the West Coast to rural Northern New England so that I could begin a job at Dartmouth College. Like many newcomers to this beautiful, resource-filled, and politically progressive area, we arrived bright-eyed and optimistic about making the Upper Valley our long-term home—comfortable, knowable, *ours*.

That coming to feel at home in this new environment might prove more difficult than we had assumed was perhaps foreshadowed by our first encounter with the older white couple who lived next door. Eager to make their acquaintance, we stepped off the front porch onto our picturesque street lined with towering chestnut trees and colorful Victorian homes to introduce ourselves. In response, these longtime residents of the town asked what they probably considered an innocent question: "What is your last name?" A little taken aback, we found it hard not to see this question about our heritage—about who "our people" were—as prompted by the fact that, although I am white, my husband and children identify as Filipino American. In the years since, even though I, as a professor, and my husband, as a physician assistant, have found our life here generally quite welcoming and satisfying, my family members have also faced numerous instances that have made them question whether they actually belonged in the community we had looked forward to making our home.

Sometimes these exclusionary reminders have been subtle, such as when my husband would look out over a crowd and point out that he was the only non-white person there. Other times, they have been more blatant, such as when a peer at school told my daughter she had "Ch**k eyes" and a friend wrote in her yearbook, "Don't eat my dog," or when my husband showed up at the elementary school to collect my daughter for an appointment and the teacher sent the wrong child to the office—the only other non-white girl in her class. Then there was the patient who repeatedly arrived for his medical visits with my husband wearing a shirt emblazoned with a large Confederate flag, or the time a friend of ours laughingly and matter-of-factly recounted that a contractor doing some work at his house had referred to my husband as a "Chinaman." These and numerous similar experiences have regularly and clearly communicated to my family members that they, as non-white people, are viewed as out of place in the Upper Valley—that they are not valued for who they are as individuals but prejudged as categorically different and hence less worthy of belonging because of their non-white racial identity.

These discomfiting situations have made me want to better understand how a community that on the surface appeared to be an ideal one—highly educated, politically progressive, environmentally green, and socially tight-knit—for launching our careers and raising our children has nonetheless managed to reproduce racial inequality to such an extent that we sometimes consider leaving. To this task I have also brought my training and research as a race scholar who brings mixed methodology to bear on sociological questions about racial integration and community. Applying the techniques and perspectives I had developed in my previous research on racially diverse urban neighborhoods to the rural Upper Valley, I began what would become a multi-year research project by interviewing people of color who had moved to the region in hopes of gaining a more systematic understanding of their daily experiences and feelings as they navigated the social and cultural landscape of rural whiteness that is the Upper Valley.

In this effort to better understand how the disparities in worth and membership I and my family were witnessing had developed in this particular setting, I conducted a series of in-depth interviews with fifty-eight community members who identified as non-white. Those interviews included questions about why the respondents had chosen to move to the area and how comfortable and integrated into their new communities they felt, the latter included asking them about how many people they knew in the community, whether they felt at home there, whether they felt valued by others in the community, what social networks they had formed within the community, and whether they envisioned staying in the region long-term. Mirroring the multiracial, multinational, and professional makeup of most newcomers to the area, 62 percent of the people of color who shared their stories with me were Asian American, while only 7 percent were Latino American. Although the relative proportion of these two groups is atypical of most rural areas in the US, they reflect the way in which the Upper Valley's employment context is dominated by education, healthcare, and technology sectors that often recruit from a global workforce and capitalize on immigration policies that favor highly educated workers. (See the Methodological Appendix for a detailed description of the study's data-collection and analytic approach and participant demographics.)

As a result of my initial analysis of those interviews, I also began to wonder how cognizant the white residents on the other side of this equation actually were of the racial changes that had been taking place in their communities and how they viewed those changes. Although I was aware that much of the existing literature on racial change in rural areas had found that such shifts often left local white residents feeling threatened and overwhelmed, it was not clear to me whether the same was true in the Upper Valley. To uncover just how noticeable the still relatively small proportion of racial minorities had become to long-term white residents or if those residents viewed these newcomers' mostly professional occupational status as a threat to their own social mobility or position, I expanded my research to include a survey of residents living in four towns in the Upper Valley. This survey (which asked respondents whether they were aware of changes in the racial makeup of their town, what observations they may have made about the impact of such changes, and whether they believed that newcomers should adapt to the local culture or feel free to practice their own) yielded responses from 147 white residents of the area. Although the experiences and beliefs of those white respondents were not the central focus of this study, their answers to these questions provided invaluable information for interpreting and understanding the reported experiences of the non-white individuals I interviewed.

What I would learn from my interviews with the people of color who had moved to this rural community in Northern New England was perhaps best typified by the experiences and feelings of Saanvi, an immigrant from India who lived and worked as a family medicine physician in rural Vermont. Saanvi had been ecstatic when, fresh out of her residency program, she received an offer to work in the Upper Valley, as it would allow her to reunite with her husband, a mechanical engineer who had already moved to the area for a job at a software company, and to work in a medically underserved area for three years and thereby waive the immigration requirement that she return to India after her medical training. Seven years later, Saanvi was still working at that hospital and reported loving her job, the natural beauty and four seasons of the area, and the many benefits that rural life offered her growing family. Her young son attended a great public elementary school, and she was comforted to live in a country with less government corruption than the one she had left. When I asked her if she felt like she had become part of the community, however, she paused, and the rising inflection of her eventual response—"Certainly?"— made her sound much less certain than she had apparently intended, leading her to laugh in seeming embarrassment.

From there, her tone quickly turned serious as she described a number of encounters that had left her feeling like she still did not quite belong. She reported, for instance, that when, in her work as a physician, she would call patients at their homes to discuss test results or treatment plans, many would respond to her accented English by hanging up before she could get in more than a few words, which she assumed meant they had mistaken her for a telemarketer or customer service representative. At other times, patients who were angry with her for not being able to give them what they wanted—such as pain medication refills—had yelled at her, "Go back to your country!" Although Saanvi had been heartened to find that "once my patients get to know me, they love me," she admitted that such incidents had taken a toll and "during hard times, I ask myself: Why am I still here?"

Saanvi's uncertainty about whether to remain in the area was also prompted by what she perceived as more subtle slights from others in the community. In one such incident, the staff in a local restaurant had directed her and her husband away from a table in the main area and toward one in a corner, which they interpreted as an attempt to hide their presence from other customers, so they chose to leave and dine somewhere else. In another example, she and her husband noticed that the reports they received about their son's day when they picked him up from daycare did not seem as full as those given to other parents, and after he repeatedly came home with bite and scratch marks that the staff couldn't explain, they decided to move him to another school. Saanvi appeared disappointed, frustrated, and worn down by these repeated exclusions, which she described as evidence that other people in her community didn't see her as valuable in the same ways she saw herself. Still, she remained because of a lukewarm sense of hope for a better future: "Maybe it will change. I don't know. We feel like we are living in limbo."

Both the hopes and disappointments expressed in the stories of Saanvi and other residents of color I interviewed appeared to be a result of the paradoxical nature of the Upper Valley, which shares many of the characteristics of both rural and urban areas and is home to substantial populations of both very poor and very wealthy residents. Tucked between the Green and White Mountains in the northeastern Appalachian Range, the Upper Valley comprises a group of small towns clustered along both sides of the Connecticut River, which marks the border between Vermont and New Hampshire. While the area is technically defined as rural and its small towns certainly feel bucolic and charming, the Upper Valley is also home to the kind of "eds and meds" institutions—colleges and hospitals—that characterize many of the country's largest and most financially successful cities.[1] Further, unlike the population shifts in the diversifying rural areas in the Midwest and South that have been the major focus of the burgeoning "new destinations" literature in the social sciences, most of the people of color who have moved to the Upper Valley have been actively recruited to fulfill specialized occupational roles in healthcare, higher education, software development, and engineering and thus occupy a structural position of equal or even higher economic and educational status than many of the longtime white residents of the area.[2]

The availability of these high-status professional jobs has led to substantial socioeconomic inequality within and among the small towns that make up the larger Upper Valley region. While some of those towns are thriving, others have been economically left behind, reflecting a broader trend in rural America in which technological change and globalization over the second half of the twentieth century have led to a steady deterioration in the demand for manufacturing and agricultural labor and to what other analysts have described as a brain drain and a hollowing out of the young white population (Carr and Kefalas 2009). Along with such declines among their population, some Upper Valley towns have been unable to support important local businesses, like grocery stores and essential public services.

According to the information gathered by my interviews, the recent influx of people with high professional status in the Upper Valley bears some similarities with what other scholars have termed *lifestyle* or *amenity migration*, in which affluent urbanites are drawn to the recreational opportunities and relaxed lifestyle offered by certain rural places and choose to move permanently or purchase a second home there. Other once-declining rural places that have successfully shifted their economies to modern extractive industries (e.g., fracking) have found that such economic windfalls can be accompanied by social challenges when longtime working-class residents find themselves priced out of their existing properties in a booming housing market and excluded from the changing cultural community.[3] Whether such newcomers come for the lifestyle or the job, the substantial in-migration of highly educated and more affluent people to struggling rural places has contributed to what sociologists have termed *rural gentrification*, in which higher-status newcomers assert their cultural and economic power to marginalize and/or displace longtime residents (Pilgeram 2021). As these sweeping structural and cultural transformations have affected both the personal livelihoods and community standing of working-class rural white people, many have internalized a divisive political rhetoric that describes them as being left behind by others who "cut in line" on their way to the American Dream (Hochschild 2018).

Despite the particularities of the situation in the Upper Valley, its accelerating racial diversity nonetheless reflects many of the broader demographic changes occurring in rural places across the country.[4] Northern New England as a whole—generally defined as including the nation's three whitest states: Maine, Vermont, and New Hampshire—has experienced noticeable racial change in recent decades. Between 1990 and 2017, the non-white population of the region jumped by 144 percent (Chiumenti 2020) and the number of racialized minority residents in the Upper Valley nearly quadrupled. As racial and ethnic minorities have been moving to the region, many white residents have moved away or passed away, further reducing their percentage of the population.

As previous scholars have observed, the in-migration of non-white residents can serve as a "demographic lifeline" for socioeconomically struggling rural communities as newcomers open small businesses, boost school enrollments, and provide essential workers to offset the vacancies left by declines in the white population (Lichter, Parisi, and Taquino 2018). Despite the important role they have often played in economically sustaining the communities of the white residents who remain, those racial demographic changes have also exposed those residents to people of color as neighbors, coworkers, and schoolmates, perhaps for the first time. As a result, according to researchers who have taken a closer look at such rural communities, the economic and institutional benefits of such diversification have also often been accompanied by a solidifying of social boundaries (Lichter and Brown 2011) and an increase in exclusionary policies geared toward racial and ethnic minorities, who have frequently been cast by others in those communities as "takers" or invaders (Ehrkamp and Nagel 2014). As history and recent events have amply demonstrated, previously unseen increases in the number of people of color moving into traditionally white places inevitably lead to tensions around who gets to define the dominant culture of the area, often expressed as white fears of an imagined "rising tide of color" that is seen as threatening white culture and supremacy worldwide.[5] Such evidence suggests that perhaps especially in diversifying communities in which local status hierarchies are disrupted by the arrival of people of color with relatively equal or higher socioeconomic status, white residents are likely to respond to feelings of status threat by attempting to hold on to their long-held power to set the cultural standards of the community.

Indeed, the information gathered for this study clearly indicates that in the Upper Valley, as elsewhere, absent political and institutional forms of discrimination that keep people of color from achieving the benefits of full membership in what has traditionally been a white space, longtime white residents frequently employ cultural means to maintain their assumed position at the top of the racial status hierarchy. As this book will argue and the following chapters will demonstrate, the principal mechanism by which white residents of the Upper Valley have attempted to maintain their social position and keep people of color "in their place" at a lower tier of that hierarchy is *misrecognition*—a failure or unwillingness to see people of color as legitimate, welcome, and valuable members of the community, as "one of us."[6] Although the manifestations of misrecognition reported by the people of color I interviewed varied in form and degree of explicitness or subtlety, the cumulative effect was a wave of reminders that they were viewed as less valuable and worthy of inclusion than the white residents of the communities in which they lived. Although all of these interviewees had managed to develop a set of coping mechanisms that allowed them to maintain a certain level of equanimity, personal satisfaction, and social connection, the need to do so constituted a set of emotional and social burdens that was not imposed upon their white counterparts. The ultimate impact of such misrecognition on the people of color who participated in this study was a profound sense of what this book refers to as *homesickness,* a deep longing for a place in which one can feel safe, wanted, and accepted for who one truly is. Without such a sense of home, many of my respondents experienced a range of emotional harms that left them, like

FIGURE 0.1. **Conceptual model of the book's argument**

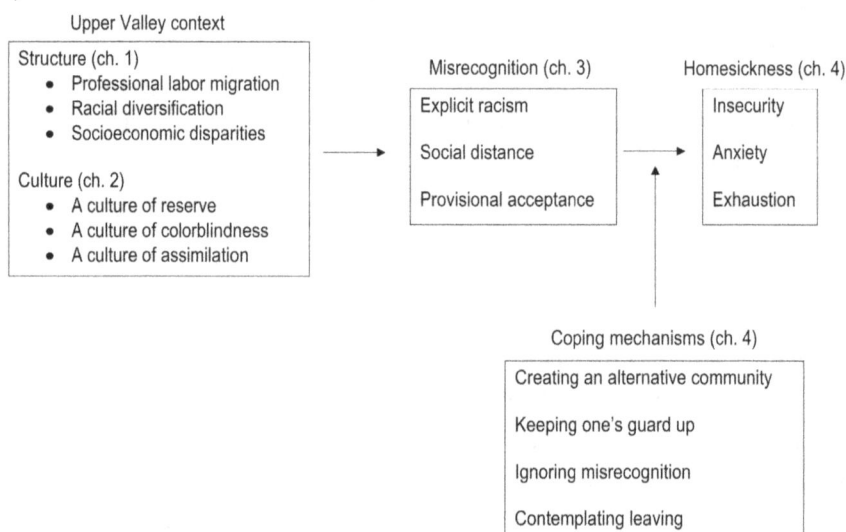

Saanvi, with a lingering unease that made it difficult for them to believe that they could ever really be at home in the rural place to which they had moved with such high hopes.

This book thus tells the story of one rural area's struggle with racial diversification, with the hope that better understanding the ways in which that effort has gone wrong for both the residents of color and the community as a whole will help identify community social interventions capable of producing a more equitable future. To accomplish this goal, the chapters follow the path of the conceptual model laid out in figure 0.1. Chapters 1 and 2 provide a portrait of the structural and the cultural environments in which the misrecognition reported by residents of the Upper Valley has developed and accrued meaning. Chapter 3 identifies and analyzes the specific mechanisms through which misrecognition works to subordinate and marginalize people of color living in this white rural environment. Chapter 4 investigates the primary symptoms of the homesickness described by my informants as a result of misrecognition and the strategies they report having developed to cope with it. The conclusion offers some empirically grounded strategies that residents and leaders of such diversifying areas might take to imagine and build a more racially equitable future for all who make a home in them.

The goals of this book, therefore, are to lay bare the particular structural and cultural factors that provide the context for racial diversification in this rural setting, to tease out the details of the misrecognition mechanisms through which white dominance is maintained, to understand how this unequal racial hierarchy gains meaning in the emotional lives of people of color, and to evaluate the possibilities for a racially equitable future in this and other diversifying places. As many small towns in rural places across the country grapple with the challenges of racial diversification, they face a choice: whether to perpetuate racial hierarchy or to disrupt it. By digging deep into the processes through which racial and ethnic minorities have been excluded from the comforts of home in one particular place, my hope is that this book can help us better understand how to recognize and unsettle those processes in diversifying spaces in general.

ONE

A Socioeconomic and Demographic Portrait of the Upper Valley

Given the Upper Valley's image as a peaceful, bucolic, and, for the most part, politically liberal place to live, many residents were shocked in late August 2017 when in Claremont, New Hampshire, an eight-year-old biracial boy was airlifted to a nearby hospital for treatment of serious injuries. A group of white teenagers had pushed the boy off a picnic table with a rope tied to an overhanging tree branch around his neck. Coming just a week after the much publicized and violent white power demonstration in Charlottesville, Virginia, this incident was interpreted by many in the community as an attempted lynching.

That interpretation was initially supported by reports that earlier in the day, the same teens had been yelling "White Pride" and calling the biracial boy the n-word while throwing rocks and sticks at him. Later accounts added that the teens involved had been playing a game in which they had taken turns jumping up on a picnic table and putting a rope from an old tire swing around their own necks before telling the boy to do the same, at which time one of the teens pushed him off the table and left the boy to swing back and forth before he managed to remove the rope and dropped to the ground. Whatever the teens' actual intentions, the Claremont police chief initially described the incident as an "accident" and downplayed racism as an explanation, saying the white teens "needed to be protected" and that their "mistakes" should not have to follow them for the rest of their lives (Hauser and Seelye 2017).

Two weeks later, after the incident had attracted viral social media outrage and national news coverage, the police opened an investigation into the possibility that this was a racially motivated hate crime. In a subsequent public statement, the police chief seemed to blame the incident—or at least the uproar it had unleashed—on recent national racial unrest and described it simply as evidence that Claremont was "not immune to anything going on in the rest of the country" (Guerra and Andersen 2017). Some white members of the community appeared to take umbrage at the accusations of racism, including the mother of the teen accused of pushing the boy off the table. In an interview with *Newsweek*, she claimed that her family had been the victim of retaliatory hate crimes by members of the community because of their presumed racism (Seaton 2017). And when a number of town residents organized a candlelight vigil to express their dismay and sadness over what to them appeared to be a blatant and violently racist event in their community, they were met by a truckload of white men driving by waving a Confederate flag and loudly mocking the "Black Lives Matter" slogan.

Two years later, following a state-level investigation, the New Hampshire attorney general's office reported that it had found "no reliable evidence that any child used racist terminology in conjunction with the rope incident, and no reasonable inference to be made in that regard" and therefore declared the teens' actions "not a hate crime" and decided against taking any civil rights action (Valley News 2019). Still, in response to this particular incident and the increased nationwide awareness of racial inequities spurred by the murder of George Floyd in 2020, several Upper Valley towns instituted racial justice committees in an attempt to acknowledge and hold people and institutions accountable for racial inequities within the region. Despite the many public declarations of racial tolerance by representatives of those communities and private claims of solidarity with residents of color by many white residents, heated discussions in town meetings and on town listserv groups have continued to reveal an undercurrent of unease with the inexorable racial diversification taking place in the Upper Valley.

To better understand these divergent reactions and how an event that many people perceived as an overtly racist hate crime—an alleged lynching attempt of a biracial boy—could have taken place in a rural community that many residents would describe as a nearly ideal place to live, this chapter examines shifts in the demographic and socioeconomic environment of the Upper Valley, which have made it not only less homogeneously white but also increasingly different from that familiar to longtime residents just a few decades ago. Although, as noted in the introduction, most of the area's new residents of color had been actively recruited to help fill a growing number of well-paid jobs and had based their decision to move there on the same lifestyle benefits valued by longtime residents, they also brought different experiences, tastes, and expectations that, as we shall see throughout this book, sometimes seemed to put them at odds with their new environment and their largely white and often less-affluent neighbors. Even though most of these newcomers were not directly competing with many longtime residents for the same jobs, their growing numbers and higher incomes had noticeably increased competition and prices for homes in the area, leading at least some of their neighbors to begin to feel pushed out of their hometowns. To some longtime residents, the differing cultural backgrounds, values, and practices of the newcomers also appeared to exacerbate social and political divisions between not only white and non-white residents but residents of the more- and less-affluent communities within the region.

As this chapter will show, interactions between longtime white residents and the newer residents of color attempting to create new lives and negotiate their right to belong in their Upper Valley communities have been shaped both by the motivations and expectations of those newcomers and by shifts in the economies and demographics of the small towns across the area, which have impacted new and old residents alike. To illuminate the context in which those interactions have taken place, the chapter first examines the factors that motivated and shaped these newcomers' decision to make a home for themselves and their families in the Upper Valley. It then explores the geographic, demographic, and socioeconomic factors that have shaped their lives and their reception within the Upper Valley as a whole, followed by a more fine-grained examination of how those impacts have varied in three representative towns in the region. As this analysis reveals, a distinctive set of structural inequalities within the region has contributed to the feeling among newcomers of being unwelcome and not worthy of full membership in the area they had chosen to make a home.

The Quest for the Good Life in the Upper Valley

Although the Upper Valley shares many of the characteristics of other rural areas across the country, the area is perhaps unique in the nature and scope of the lifestyles and opportunities it offers to the people who live there. Socioeconomically, the area is home to both a substantial proportion of residents who are barely escaping poverty and many who can count themselves among the nation's one-percenters (which in 2023 meant having a household income above $652,657).[1] While the area's natural setting allows residents to participate in a wide range of outdoor activities, such as hiking or fishing, during the day, the many cultural opportunities available in its towns also make it possible to attend a theatrical or dance production in the evening. Nestled as it is between two segments of the Appalachian Mountain range, the Upper Valley is indisputably a rural area, but it also sits just a few hours' drive from major metropolitan areas, including Boston, Montreal, and New York. And according to the responses of the newcomers I interviewed, it is precisely this distinctive nexus of resources and opportunities that has drawn increasing numbers of young professional people of color to move to the Upper Valley to advance their careers and raise their families.

Among the people of color I interviewed, most reported having relocated to the Upper Valley principally to advance their careers and to also provide their families with access to the area's excellent public schools and high-quality housing. But another major theme that emerged from these interviewees' responses was that they had viewed the Upper Valley as a place that would allow them to have what they described as "the best of both worlds." According to Hayden, a young Black professional who had lived in the area for five years, the Upper Valley offered residents not only a quaint, "quintessential New England" environment full of small "towns where you can still see the big white church buildings right on the green, horses, people gardening, and things like that" but "also an intellectual center" that provides many of the cultural advantages typically associated with more urban settings. Zayyan, an Indonesian physician who had moved to the area fifteen years earlier, described that bimodal character of the Upper Valley as making it an especially good place for raising a family and for advancing a successful medical career: "Of course, there are fewer people out here. It is an open space. It is safe and better for younger families. Those were my main reasons. But it furthered my career as well. In [the city from which he had moved], a lot of people have my [medical] specialty. Here, I was the only one in the area. It makes a difference in terms of being a big fish in a small pond, rather than a fry in the sea."

A number of interviewees specifically reported choosing life in the rural Upper Valley over a variety of other options available to them because they viewed it as a calm environment free of many of the hassles and pressures that often come with urban life. Suresh, who was originally from India but at the time of our interview had lived in the region twenty-seven years, perhaps summed up this feeling most simply, describing his town as a "pleasant" and "quiet" place where "everything seems to work more easily than elsewhere." Ehsan, a South Asian physician who had lived in the Upper Valley for sixteen years, also appreciated that area residents appeared less focused on matters of status and prestige than those in the cities in which he had lived, where people would "immediately ask, 'What do you do for a living?'" City dwellers appeared most concerned "about their career, their kids, their job, where they want to go," he said. "They have a lot of frustration for some reason. I think a lot of people are struggling in [the city], but here, they are calm people. They are settled down. They are very happy." Steven, a young Black professional who had moved to the Upper Valley seven years earlier, particularly valued that, in his earlier life in the city, he had "literally choreographed my life around traffic. Now I never think about that. Never do I wake up and think, 'How am I going to get to my job and avoid traffic?' I just get in my car and drive on over here." Samuel, a sixty-five-year-old Haitian man, reported moving to the area specifically to escape the kind of stress that had previously pervaded his life: "The main reason I moved up here was peace of mind. I got out of the military, which was very disturbing—in terms of the war, the gunshot wounds, the ambulances, the shootings. So, I decided I needed a peaceful place to stay. Vermont was suggested, and it ended up being exactly what I wanted. I moved up here in 2003, and I have been here since. It has been wonderful."

A number of these interviewees of color reported having moved to the

Upper Valley specifically to enjoy the benefits of being surrounded by nature and easy access to the outdoors. Eunice, a Korean American, recounted having been inspired to move to the Upper Valley sixteen years earlier by her visits to the area with her family while she was growing up: "We originally moved to Vermont because we had come here for vacations. I wanted to live in a co-housing community on this organic farm, so my kids could run around and have chickens and play with cows and all that kind of stuff." Shenqing, who had grown up in China and moved to the Upper Valley six years earlier, reported that he had also earlier vacationed in the area while working as a biotech researcher in a nearby city and had decided to move there specifically to take advantage of the outdoor opportunities it offered and to pass on his love of nature to his children. "I came here as soon as I got my green card. I just couldn't wait. We had come to see the foliage every single year. We loved New Hampshire. When I was a kid, my father would take me hunting, and that was one of the sweetest memories of my life." Anthony, a young Black professional who had been living in the Upper Valley for three years, appreciated the rural setting's calming effect on his mind: "It is very quiet and has a lot of hidden gems. It also makes you realize how peaceful nature can be. There are definitely some positives. It gives you a lot of time if you want to get away from everybody and not be bothered. This is the perfect place to collect your thoughts, get in deep thought." Camila, who described herself as Afro-Latina, had been recruited to the Upper Valley for a high-profile job a few years earlier, claimed she had ultimately based her decision to move to the area by its "accessibility to the outdoors, the walk to work, the scenery, the calmness, the clean air. Those things are huge for me in this stage of my life. There is no pollution; there isn't any trash; it's clean."

Another attraction of the area mentioned by a number of these residents was the civility and sense of trust that they associated with small-town living, a response to the area that several described as being shared by visiting friends and family members. According to Teresa, a Latina professional who had lived in the Upper Valley for nine years, "My friends think it is wonderful! Because in Latin America we have walls around the houses. My friends are always surprised that there are no walls and 'anyone can steal from you!' It's like a statement that everything is really organized and clean. They feel this is a very well-run, very functional place." Fu, a Chinese American who had been living in his town for eleven years, shared a similar story about a friend who had visited from a nearby city: "He was so surprised. We had to work during the day, so he basically drove around the White Mountains on his own. He passed a farm and there was nobody there, but there was a booth with blueberries and a sign saying '$5 per Bucket.' He had no idea that this can happen. He just took a bucket and put in five dollars." Several respondents cited the courteous way in which most people drive as an example of what they viewed as the kindness of people in these small towns, such as Fu's observation that "when you are in a big city, people don't stop for you when you cross the street. But here, everybody does that. It is so much nicer." Shenqing offered what he considered a particularly telling story about such small-town civility: "It was like 5:00 or 6:00 p.m., like rush time—everyone was going back home. I was new here. I stopped at a stop sign, and I think I was daydreaming. I was waiting for a traffic light or something. It was maybe like half a minute later when I woke up. I looked behind me and there were maybe a dozen cars waiting there. Yeah, they were just sitting there, nobody honked. This would be impossible in [the city]. I was so moved!"

Even though most of the residents of color I interviewed were generally satisfied with their decision to move to the Upper Valley, they also seemed well aware that it had its downsides and that not everyone was likely to agree with their choice. Frances, an ethnically Chinese woman who had grown up in the Philippines and had been living in the Upper Valley for fifteen years, reported that not all her visitors had a positive impression of her new home, such as a friend who "could not see the beauty of the place. I kept saying, 'Isn't it nice? Isn't it nice?' And she was like, 'Why did you move here? It is so damn cold.' It is a little bit more rural, a little bit more quiet, so it's not necessarily what they would have chosen themselves. I would say a lot of my friends would not want to live here." Katie, an Indonesian woman who had lived in the Upper Valley for fifteen years, reported that her parents had visited "a couple times and they didn't like it at all. My mom said, 'Wow, you don't see your neighbors. You don't see people.'" Xiu, a young Chinese woman who had moved to the Upper Valley to accept a temporary postdoctoral position, laughed as she recounted that, as her parents were leaving after a visit, "I was like, 'Oh, Mom, I'm so happy you are here, and I am going to invite you back soon, so we can spend some time together.' And my mom said, 'Well, I think the next time we come is when you get moved to a better location!'"

A few interviewees' descriptions of their decision to move to the Upper Valley seemed to echo the more negative responses of such visitors. Jocelyn, a Filipina American who had lived in her small town for four years, admitted to being rather unprepared for the different lifestyle she faced after moving there for a professional opportunity:

> I applied on a whim. I didn't know where New Hampshire was. It was only when they sent me the ticket that I looked it up on a map. And I was like, "Wow, I didn't realize the US was shaped that way." But I decided to do it. What I found is that I didn't account for the non-job part of it. If you asked me soon after I moved here what I liked doing, my answer for a while was that I liked going out to new restaurants and I liked hanging out in coffee shops and I liked sitting in a park and reading. You know what, none of those things are possible here. I didn't quite understand what this place was for a very long time because all my anchors didn't have a directly translatable counterpart here.

Ayana, a young Black professional in her first year in the area, reported spending a lot of time thinking about things she missed from her previous lifestyle, especially Black-owned businesses, "not just for food, clothing, and culture, but necessities like hair care. I can't tell you how difficult it is as a Black woman. I have to travel hundreds of miles to find somebody who can appropriately and healthily work through my hair. It is really disheartening." Fei, a Chinese American woman who had also lived in her town for only a year, admitted, "When I was moving here, I didn't realize quite how isolated it was. I had a slightly more idealized vision of New Hampshire and Vermont, with idyllic scenery. It is beautiful here, but it gets very dark in winter, and it is very isolated. There is like one grocery store and no reception on my phone or anything." Although the less-than-positive responses of those particular interview participants might be attributed largely to their being relatively new to the area and still actively comparing their new environment to the more populous and diverse places in which they had previously lived, they also hint at some of the harder realities faced by people of color attempting to build satisfying lives and to be accepted as full members of such predominantly white spaces as the Upper Valley.

Demographic and Economic Differences
Within the Upper Valley

Although the term *Upper Valley* (a reference to the Upper Connecticut River Valley) was first coined in 1952 by the local newspaper, the *Valley News*, to differentiate its coverage area from that of its nearest competitor just south along the river, the name has since become common usage among local residents, businesses, and institutions. Whereas the specific geographic boundaries of the area have been drawn somewhat differently by various local agencies and organizations, this book has adopted the newspaper's current operating definition, which includes forty-six towns arranged along a forty-mile stretch of the Connecticut River that separates Vermont from New Hampshire, as shown in map 1.1.[2]

According to Upper Valley residents' online responses to geographer Garrett Dash Nelson's invitation to draw and comment upon their conceptions of the region's boundaries, many hold a rather more nebulous sense of the geographic scope and identity of the area, one based less on formal borders than on their sense of home and familiarity.[3] Yet Nelson's data did reveal an important distinction that many respondents appeared to make between different areas within the region, resulting in a general consensus that four particular towns—Lebanon and Hanover in New Hampshire and Norwich and Hartford in Vermont—constitute the core of the Upper Valley, surrounded by other towns at its periphery. This widespread perception, which also appeared consistent with the responses of many of the residents interviewed for this study, was undoubtedly based not simply on those four towns' geographical location at the center of the region but on their being the site of 44 percent of the region's jobs (McDermott and Work 2019). That those towns constitute the major employment hub of the region is largely a result of their being home to two major institutions: an Ivy League university, Dartmouth College, and a large regional medical center, Dartmouth Health. In addition to those institutions' employing more than 17,000 individuals, the professional schools affiliated with Dartmouth College have also stimulated the establishment of

MAP 1.1. **Map of the Upper Valley, 2024.**

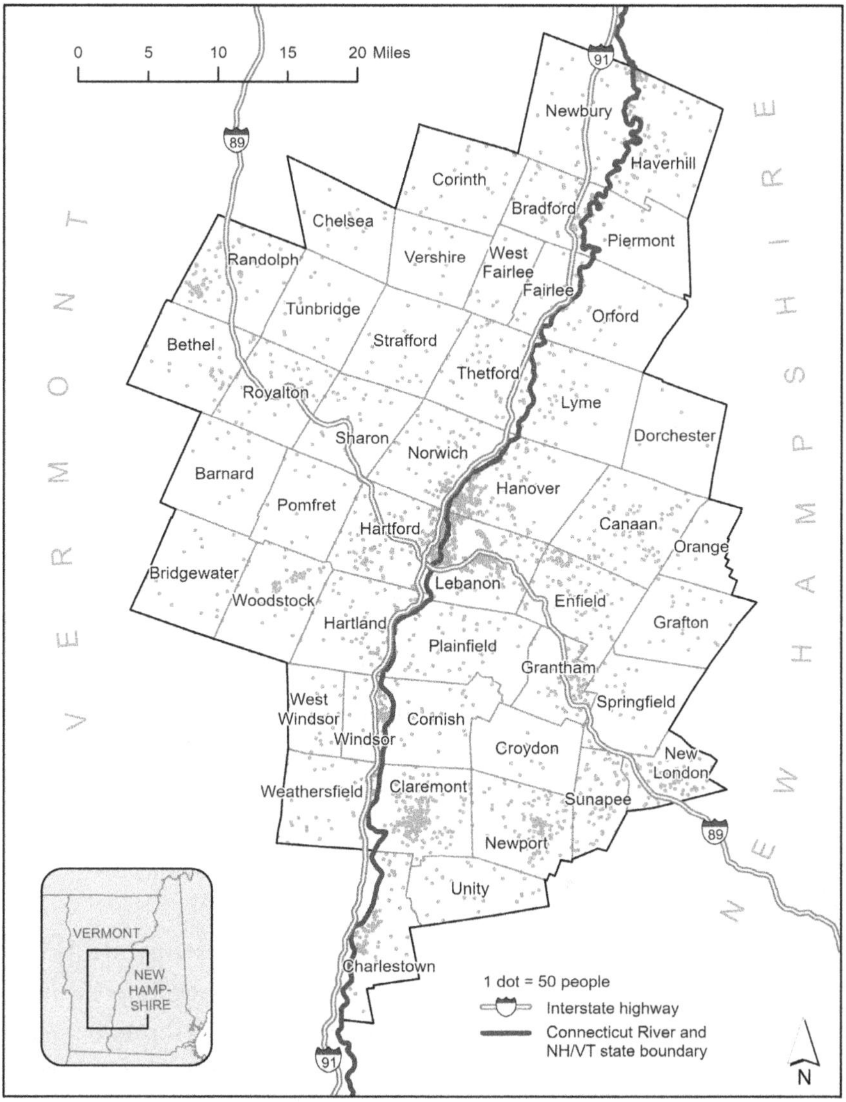

Created by Jonathan W. Chipman, Citrin Family GIS/Applied Spatial Analysis Lab, Dartmouth College.

numerous high-tech and entrepreneurial startups within or near that core (Ragsdale 2018). Though the quality of life and the economics of the core and the periphery are obviously intertwined, the responses gathered by Nelson also reflect a perceived social hierarchy between the two areas, most notably in an apparent sense of self-importance among residents of the core and of resentment from those living outside what one commenter sardonically described as the "center of the universe." Additional evidence of a social divide within the region was provided by comments from residents of the core that described the more peripheral towns as "iffy" places to live and their residents as deserving only "partial credit" as members of the Upper Valley.

As those comments suggest, that distinction between the two areas is based not simply on their relative geographical locations but on demographic and economic differences between them, the most dramatic of which has been the uneven population growth and decline among towns within the Upper Valley. Between 1990 and 2020, the core towns with economies based on educational, technological, and healthcare services experienced substantial population growth that, birth and death data indicate, was primarily attributable to in-migration. Those increases led in turn to a serious housing crunch within the core towns, sparking increased competition for housing, rising home prices, and population spread to nearby towns. As a result, towns once considered part of the "outer banks" of the Upper Valley have since come to be viewed by many as bedroom communities serving the professionals employed in the core. Most recently, the housing crunch in the core of the Upper Valley has been further worsened by a pandemic-inspired wave of migration of wealthy urbanites to such rural destinations, mirroring a rural gentrification trend that has led to a dramatic increase in the volume and price of home sales across rural Northern New England (Nelson and Frost 2022).

In marked contrast to those developments within the core, the populations of the towns in the periphery, especially the former mill towns in the more southern and northern reaches of the valley, continued to shrink over that period. Although, as discussed in more detail below, those population declines were largely a result of an economic shift from manufacturing to service industries within the region, they also reflect the impact of successful lobbying efforts by powerful state leaders in the 1960s to locate the junction of two major interstate highways (I-89 and I-91) at the heart of what have become its core towns, effectively cutting off the more distant sections of the Upper Valley from the social and economic development that has helped make the core the attractive destination for professional migrants that it has become today. The increasingly obvious socioeconomic inequality between the core and periphery and increases in property taxes resulting from the spread of high-income new residents across the region as a whole have led to increased economic stress and feelings of exclusion among many of the longtime residents of such towns.

Further complicating some long-term white residents' response to the diverging class fortunes among Upper Valley towns is that most of the population growth in the area during this period has been the result of increases in the number of Asian American, Black, Latino, and multiracial residents of the area. As figure 1.1 reveals, during the last full decade for which census data are available, more than three quarters of the towns in the Upper Valley experienced a decline in white population, while the non-white population of all but one of those towns increased by double- or even triple-digit percentages.[4] Those shifts in the racial makeup of the population of the Upper Valley have been in sync, if a bit delayed, with what demographers have recognized as one of the most dramatic national population shifts in recent history, in which rural areas and small towns have seen increasing numbers of white residents leave and people of color arrive, thereby transforming the social and structural fabric of those places.[5]

Yet a closer look at the census data also reveals variations in that pattern of increasing racial diversity within individual towns in the Upper Valley. The complex socioeconomic and demographic context of the area and its varying impacts on the experiences and reception of newcomers of color can be seen in a comparison of three towns: Claremont and Hanover in New Hampshire and Hartford in Vermont. These particular locations were selected because they have populations that are relatively large compared to those of other Upper Valley towns and reflect the range of economic and social environments across the area. Even though the Upper Valley's many small towns, most with fewer than a few thousand residents, are vital to the area's identity and sense of place, the people of color who are the main concern of this book tend to have less reason to live in or to visit them often. Representing the varied socioeconomic

FIGURE 1.1. Percent change in racial populations of Upper Valley towns, 2010-2020.

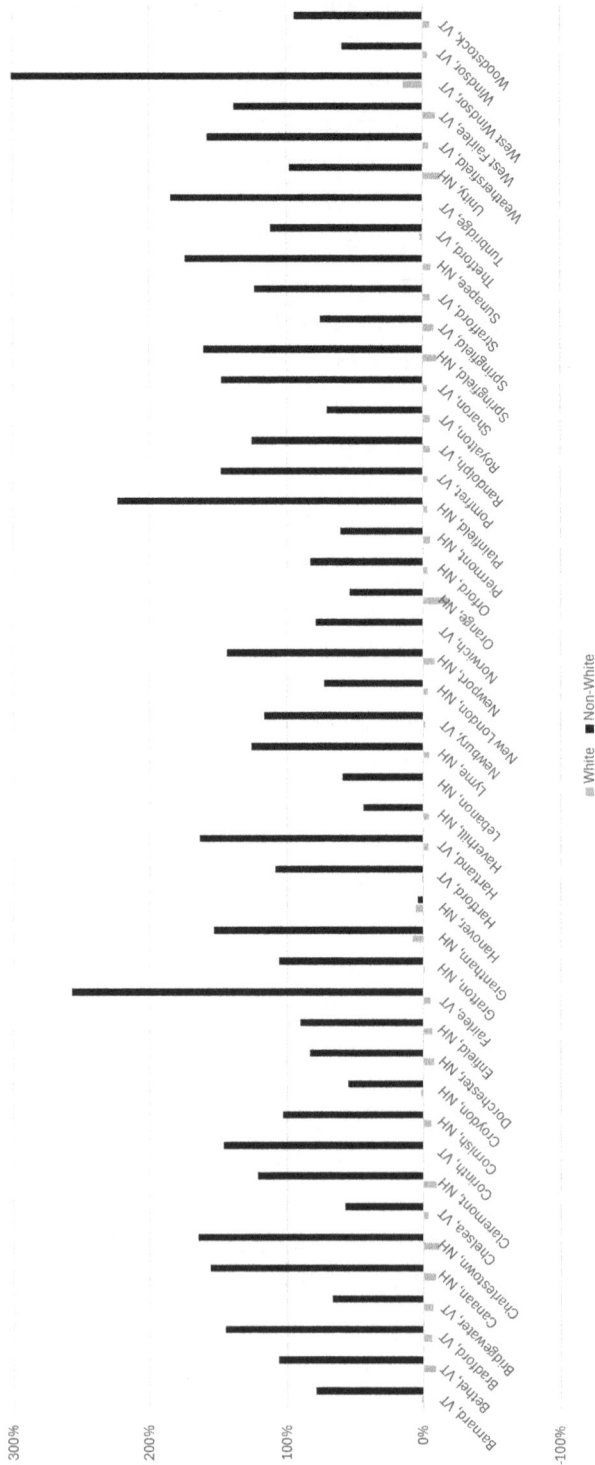

Barnard, VT
Bethel, VT
Bridgewater, VT
Canaan, NH
Charlestown, NH
Chelsea, VT
Claremont, NH
Cornish, NH
Croydon, NH
Dorchester, NH
Enfield, NH
Fairlee, VT
Grafton, NH
Grantham, NH
Hanover, NH
Hartford, VT
Hartland, VT
Haverhill, NH
Lebanon, NH
Lyme, NH
Newbury, VT
New London, NH
Newport, NH
Norwich, VT
Orange, NH
Orford, NH
Piermont, NH
Plainfield, NH
Pomfret, VT
Randolph, VT
Royalton, VT
Sharon, VT
Springfield, VT
Strafford, VT
Sunapee, VT
Thetford, VT
Tunbridge, VT
Unity, NH
Weathersfield, VT
West Fairlee, VT
West Windsor, VT
Windsor, VT
Woodstock, VT

300%
200%
100%
0%
-100%

■ White ■ Non-White

Source: U.S. Census Bureau 2020 Census.

conditions across the area, these three locales include an economically disadvantaged community located at the periphery of the area and an affluent community and an economically mixed community within the core of the area.

Claremont, NH: A Disadvantaged Community

Claremont, the site of the incident discussed in the opening of the chapter, is a once economically thriving but currently struggling town located twenty-five miles down the Connecticut River from the core towns. Claremont was an early US colonial settlement, and its name, a reference to the grand English country estate of the British Earl of Clare, evokes its settlers' ambitious hopes for prosperity, initially through farming in the fertile lands of the Connecticut River watershed. By the mid-1800s, Claremont's economy had begun to boom as enterprising residents harnessed waterpower from the Sugar River to run its paper, machinery, cotton, and woolen textile mills, bringing considerable financial success to the town that had developed around a compact center. This earlier era of affluence remains evident in some of the prominent Victorian homes and the impressive architecture lining the once-bustling downtown square.[6] As recently as fifty years ago, Claremont had been a prime shopping and entertainment destination in the Upper Valley (O'Grady 2022); one current resident, remembered the 1960s as "those were the days" and described the dozens of small businesses and department stores that lined the downtown area (Kenyon 2016).

By the 1980s, however, Claremont had begun to fall on hard times. Following the broader shift away from domestic industrial production in the US, most of the jobs in Claremont's once-robust mill industry disappeared, leaving large numbers of residents unemployed. The previously mentioned decision to locate the intersection of two major interstate highways twenty-five miles north of Claremont led to a loss in traffic that resulted in the shuttering of many downtown storefronts. During revitalization efforts in the early 2000s, the community was able to sell several large mill buildings to private businesses, which converted them to such uses as the headquarters of a computing technology firm and a shared studio workspace for small-scale "makers" such as furniture builders and quilters (Cousineau 2022). Despite such successes and Claremont officials' continued commitment to developing housing and infrastructure to support increased foot traffic to downtown small businesses (O'Grady 2022), some longtime residents appeared dissatisfied with the focus and pace of Claremont's progress, such as one resident who, expressing dismay about the "discarded trash and drug dealing," told a reporter that what Claremont needed was not downtown revitalization but "a factory to come in and hire . . . the illiterate people that can't read or write" (Cousineau 2022).

As the data in table 1.1 suggest, such a return to Claremont's manufacturing past seems unlikely, given that over the past three decades, manufacturing's percentage of Claremont's industry dropped from 30.6 percent to just 17 percent. Even though the severe housing crisis in the Upper Valley's core towns has led to more interest in Claremont's housing market, as late as 2020 the median value of owner-occupied housing units in Claremont was just $133,400, still less than half of New Hampshire's statewide median value of $272,300. The educational attainment of its residents has risen over time but in 2020 still lagged that of the rest of the state, with only 21.2 percent of Claremont's population twenty-five years or older having attained a bachelor's degree or higher, compared to 40.2 percent in New Hampshire as a whole. Amid this socioeconomic stagnation, Claremont's total population has steadily shrunk over the previous three decades, declining by 6.9 percent between 1990 and 2020, when there were 12,949 residents. But what that percentage does not reveal by itself is that while the white population decreased by 15.4 percent over those three decades, the non-white population increased by 424.4 percent, somewhat offsetting but not fully stemming the city's population loss. While it is impossible to know for sure whether the white teenagers who pushed the biracial boy off the picnic table were acting out of racial animus or their own status anxiety, there is little doubt that they grew up in a town that currently afforded few opportunities for social mobility among its long-time white residents.

Despite that statistically dramatic racial diversification, most of which is attributable to a growing number of multiracial and Latino American residents, the actual number and percentage of non-white residents of Claremont has remained fairly small. The marked but modest nature of this change may help explain why one interviewee of color who lived in Claremont described her new home more in terms of its seeming socioeconomic disadvantage—

especially compared to other towns in the Upper Valley—than in terms of its racial diversity.[7]

> It feels like an old mill town. I would say it's much more of a middle- or low-class background. I have seen maybe a handful of people of color. But it's cute. There is a paper factory nearby and some superstores, but generally it's just houses. When I was moving there, I heard a lot about what Claremont was. A lot of the talk around it was like, "That's not a great place," and "You need to be careful on crime and your safety." I understand where some of that is coming from. But it felt like the narrative was kind of negative, to be honest. They would say, "I have not heard great things about that area," or "It's not as family oriented." And, like, "The schools aren't as good." Some of it, I think, is coded language to talk about feeling less comfortable being in an area where the socioeconomic status is so different. The messaging was like, "Especially for a woman of color, for a young woman, it's not necessarily an ideal place for living."

While this response aptly summarizes the socioeconomic and demographic situation in Claremont, it also reflects the complex interplay of race and class in both the experiences and reception of residents of color in the Upper Valley and the attitudes of residents from the core and periphery of the area toward each other, including the possible resentments of residents who may feel left behind.

TABLE 1.1. Claremont, NH: Selected sociodemographic characteristics, 1990-2020.

	1990		2000		2010		2020		% Δ '90-'20
Industry for employed persons 16 years and over									
Manufacturing	1,949	30.6%	1,826	27.8%	1,300	18.8%	1,051	17.0%	-46.1%
Education, healthcare, social services	1,096	17.2%	1,420	21.6%	1,900	27.5%	1,599	25.9%	45.9%
Median value for specified owner-occupied housing units									
	$83,300		$78,200		$151,800		$133,400		60.1%
Educational attainment for population 25 years and over									
Less than high school	2,961	32.4%	1,930	21.3%	1,141	11.8%	1,252	12.8%	
High school graduate	5,098	55.8%	5,958	65.8%	7,030	72.7%	6,453	66.0%	
Bachelor's degree or higher	1,069	11.8%	1,156	12.8%	1,503	15.5%	2,071	21.2%	93.7%
Total population									
	13,902		13,151		13,355		12,949		-6.9%

Race and ethnicity

White	13,631	98.1%	12,798	97.3%	12,713	95.2%	11,528	89.0%	-15.4%
Non-white									
Black or African American	34	0.2%	41	0.3%	81	0.6%	74	0.6%	
American Indian and Alaska Native	83	0.6%	42	0.3%	41	0.3%	57	0.4%	
Asian American	79	0.6%	81	0.6%	126	0.9%	170	1.3%	
Native Hawaiian and Pacific Islander			4	0.0%	3	0.0%	3	0.0%	
Other race	4	0.0%	5	0.0%	9	0.1%	44	0.3%	
Multiracial			114	0.9%	211	1.6%	789	6.1%	
Latino	71	0.5%	66	0.5%	171	1.3%	284	2.2%	
Total non-white	271	1.9%	353	2.7%	642	4.8%	1,421	11.0%	424.4%

Sources: U.S. Census Bureau 1990, 2000, 2010, and 2020 decennial censuses and American Community Survey (ACS) 2010 and 2020 five-year estimates.

Hanover, NH: An Affluent Community

At the other end of the region's economic spectrum lies the core town of Hanover, New Hampshire. An early colonial settlement located on the eastern
bank of the Connecticut River, Hanover's charter was originally granted by
the British royal governor of New Hampshire to colonists from Connecticut,
who named the new town after their home parish in that state. By the time
Dartmouth College was founded there eight years later in 1769, the town of
Hanover comprised about twenty families and continued to grow around
the college. In fact, the Green, which still serves as the town's social center,
is located on college property.[8] In 1893, a small hospital was also founded in
Hanover, which over time expanded into a large integrated hospital system
that eventually moved just slightly out of town into the neighboring community of Lebanon and has become the largest private employer and provider of
healthcare in the state of New Hampshire. As a result, Hanover's economic
and social identities remain tightly intertwined with a prosperous and prestigious pair of institutions.[9]

Because of its enmeshment with the college and hospital systems, Hanover's fortunes have increased over time, as evident from the census data in
table 1.2. The town's economy, long dominated by education, healthcare, and
social services, has remained remarkably stable over the past three decades, as
those sectors have continued to represent about 60 percent of the town's industry. In contrast, manufacturing, which has never been a major industry in
Hanover, represented only 2.9 percent of its economy in 1990 and declined to
just half that by 2020. Home values have also remained relatively high; in 2020
Hanover's median home value was $503,300, almost double that of the state
as a whole. As these indicators might suggest, town residents' level of educational attainment was also considerably higher than that of most residents in
the state. As of 2020, 80.5 percent of Hanover residents had attained a bachelor's degree or higher, compared to 40.2 percent of all New Hampshire residents. Clearly, many residents of the area have viewed Hanover as an attractive
place to live; during the three decades examined, Hanover's population grew
by 38.8 percent, which in this case included increases among both white and
non-white populations, though once again the percentage of those increases

was much higher among residents of color (141.5 percent) than among white residents (23.7 percent).

The descriptions of their lives in Hanover offered by the interviewees of color who lived there tended to emphasize both its affluence and its rurality, especially in contrast to other places in which they had lived. One respondent, for instance, seemed particularly aware of the obvious wealth within the town: "Where I live now, there is significant money." Another focused on the benefits of living so close to nature: "I would say that obviously it's like a picturesque college town. Outdoorsy, nature focused, you know, all four seasons. There is no pollution. And it is extremely rural. What I like is the nature-esque part and the outdoors part and the clean, fresh feel when you're outside." Yet most of those interviewees also noted the flip side of Hanover's rural nature: its lack of the kind of social vitality and racial diversity they had experienced in more urban environments. As one put it, "There's not a lot of city life, not a lot of people. I definitely will describe the diversity to be lacking. When you walk around, you don't see a whole lot of people that look like me." That so many of the respondents shared this reaction even despite Hanover's higher level of racial diversity than that of other towns in the Upper Valley is most likely explained by the town's population still remaining 77.6 percent white.

TABLE 1.2. Hanover, NH: Selected sociodemographic characteristics, 1990–2020.

	1990		2000		2010		2020		% Δ '90–'20
Industry for employed persons 16 years and over									
Manufacturing	82	2.9%	100	3.0%	48	1.4%	47	1.5%	-42.7%
Education, healthcare, social services	1,747	61.3%	2,100	62.8%	2,166	62.5%	1,877	60.0%	7.4%
Median value for specified owner-occupied housing units									
	$234,000		$248,300		$473,000		$503,300		115.1%
Educational attainment for population 25 years and over									
Less than high school	38	1.6%	137	4.1%	103	3.4%	175	4.6%	
High school graduate	429	18.5%	624	18.8%	397	13.1%	567	14.9%	
Bachelor's degree or higher	1,845	79.8%	2,554	77.1%	2,519	83.4%	3,069	80.5%	66.3%
Total population									
	6,538		8,162		8,636		9,078		38.8%

Race and ethnicity

White	5,697	87.1%	6,823	83.6%	6,412	74.3%	7,047	77.6%	23.7%
Non-white									
Black or African American	235	3.6%	181	2.2%	359	4.2%	189	2.1%	
American Indian and Alaska Native	46	0.7%	42	0.5%	82	1.0%	37	0.4%	
Asian American	410	6.3%	665	8.2%	1,069	12.4%	772	8.5%	
Native Hawaiian and Pacific Islander			7	0.1%	2	0.0%	0	0.0%	
Other race	2	0.0%	18	0.2%	17	0.2%	31	0.3%	
Multiracial			167	2.1%	296	3.4%	432	4.8%	
Latino	148	2.3%	259	3.2%	399	4.6%	570	6.3%	
Total non-white	841	12.9%	1,339	16.4%	2,224	25.8%	2,031	22.4%	141.5%

Sources: U.S. Census Bureau 1990, 2000, 2010, and 2020 decennial censuses and American Community Survey (ACS) 2010 and 2020 five-year estimates.

Hartford, VT: A Socioeconomically Mixed Community

A third variety of socioeconomic environments encountered by residents of the Upper Valley is represented by the town of Hartford, Vermont, which lies just south and across the river from its more affluent neighbor of Hanover. Hartford is one of the so-called Connecticut towns of Vermont and shares its name with the city in the nearby state.[10] The five small villages that together comprise present-day Hartford sit near the confluence of the Connecticut, White, and Ottauquechee Rivers, which earlier in the town's history had provided vital transportation and mill power.[11] In addition to the manufacturing facilitated by these advantages, residents of the area also engaged in sheep farming (for wool) and dairy farming (originally for butter and cheese and later for milk sold to factories for dairy production). The beginning of the growth of White River Junction, which has become the largest of the villages and the commercial center of Hartford, can be traced to the arrival of the railroad in 1848, which encouraged the development of related industries, hospitality services, and workforce housing.

Even though Hartford, like Hanover, is one of the Upper Valley's core towns, its prosperity, like Claremont's, also began to fade in the late twentieth century. According to one newspaper account, the growth of the interstate highway system in the 1960s eventually "siphoned away much of the town's economic lifeblood" as a transportation center, and by the 1980s the downtown that had once been the lively center of Vermont's railroad industry had turned into a "total ghost town" (Holley 2019). Nonetheless, the town's fortunes took a decided turn for the better in the 1990s when a small group of local developers, attracted to what they described as Hartford's "post-industrial vibe," invested in efforts to convert White River Junction's downtown into an artistic hub for the Upper Valley (Holley 2019). Today, this downtown area boasts two popular theater spaces, a school that teaches cartooning, and a handful of hip cafés and cocktail bars that are on regular rotation during the monthly First Friday art and music celebrations.[12] One reason the village was able to attract those development dollars was that its earlier industrial economy had revolved around the railroad rather than manufacturing, making its smaller-scale commercial buildings more amenable to downtown retail development. As one of the early investors explained, instead of having "these big, big factories in town," White River Junction "just had hotels . . . and maybe a dozen bars" (Evancie 2022). Hartford's successful rejuvenation attempts have thus been quite different from those in Claremont, which have focused primarily on attracting large companies into its factory spaces and only more recently turned to downtown commercial development.

The census data presented in table 1.3 tell a complicated story of gentrification and racial change that demonstrates both commonalities with and differences from the comparable trajectories in Claremont and Hanover. Although manufacturing in Hartford declined by 20.4 percent between 1990 and 2020, it had never accounted for as large a proportion of its industry as in many other small towns in the region and thus had a less negative effect on the livelihood of most of its residents. At the same time, the proportion of the town's residents who worked in education, healthcare, and social services grew slightly over most of that period, accounting for 33.8 percent of its industry in 2020. Home values have similarly increased, growing by 113.9 percent over the past three decades and providing evidence that many Upper Valley residents consider Hartford a desirable location. The dramatic 267.6 percent increase in the proportion of Hartford's population holding a bachelor's degree or higher over the past three decades lends credence to the widespread impression that this community has been undergoing gentrification. Bucking the general trend of population decline across the Upper Valley, Hartford's 36.8 percent growth in total population both reflects and has contributed to its economic revitalization since the 1990s. But the racial breakdown of that population growth adds a wrinkle of complexity to what might otherwise appear a straightforward story of rural gentrification: although Hartford's white population grew by 23.5 percent over that period, its non-white population grew by a remarkable 516.4 percent.

Although the experiences of the Hartford residents of color interviewed for this study varied somewhat according to the particular village in which they lived, most reported finding Hartford's rural nature more isolating than other places where they had lived. According to one respondent who lived in the village of Wilder (about a fifteen-minute walk from the revitalized downtown of White River Junction), the spread-out and largely residential nature of that community seemed to make it hard for her to connect with other residents: "I have to drive to get groceries and to get coffee and to meet friends. Here, it's

TABLE 1.3. Hartford, VT: Selected sociodemographic characteristics, 1990–2020.

	1990		2000		2010		2020		%Δ '90–'20
Industry for employed persons 16 years and over									
Manufacturing	196	8.8%	251	11.7%	112	5.6%	156	5.2%	-20.4%
Education healthcare, social services	591	26.5%	727	33.8%	518	25.9%	1,019	33.8%	72.4%
Median value for specified owner–occupied housing units									
	$103,400		$99,250		$196,431		$221,186		113.9%
Educational attainment for population 25 years and over									
Less than high school	595	21.9%	390	13.5%	351	12.1%	203	4.8%	
High school graduate	1,621	59.6%	1,851	64.2%	1,839	63.3%	2,158	51.1%	
Bachelor's degree or higher	506	18.6%	643	22.3%	716	24.7%	1,860	44.1%	267.6%
Total population									
	4,097		4,205		5,254		5,603		36.8%

Race and ethnicity

White	3,987	98.3%	4,044	96.2%	4,901	93.3%	4,925	87.9%	23.5%
Non-white								
Black or African American	15	0.4%	21	0.5%	32	0.6%	68	1.2%
American Indian and Alaska Native	15	0.4%	20	0.5%	22	0.4%	11	0.2%
Asian American	54	1.3%	32	0.8%	118	2.2%	132	2.4%
Native Hawaiian and Pacific Islander			2	0.0%	2	0.0%	1	0.0%
Other race	0	0.0%	1	0.0%	4	0.1%	11	0.2%
Multiracial			55	1.3%	105	2.0%	310	5.5%
Latino	26	0.6%	30	0.7%	70	1.3%	145	2.6%
Total non-white	110	2.7%	161	3.8%	353	6.7%	678	12.1%	516.4%

Sources: U.S. Census Bureau 1990, 2000, 2010, and 2020 decennial censuses and American Community Survey (ACS) 2010 and 2020 five-year estimates.

mostly just residents. You see a lot of people walking their dogs and old people taking walks, like after the sunset. It's really difficult for me to engage, like to talk to random people, other than my landlord next door or my downstairs neighbor." Yet even the interviewees of color who lived and worked in the more populous and busier White River Junction reported finding it hard to meet and build relationships with other residents, a problem that one viewed not as unsolvable but as requiring a more concerted effort to engage with others in the community: "White River. It's not New Jersey. It's not Boston. It's you. Are you willing to participate? Nobody invites me to the community. I just join in, say 'Hi,' and show my face. This community, for now, is my bread and butter. This is where I sleep, this is where I play, this is where I go to work." Although any newcomer might find making social connections more difficult in this low-density situation, another interviewee from White River Junction explicitly connected her sense of not "fitting in" to her impression of an over-whelming racial homogeneity among the town's residents, reporting that "it's a very interesting place, but the first thing that comes to mind is that it is a very white place. Not to say that in a negative way, but that is one of the first things that is very noticeable. Even when I had family come, they were like, 'Whoa, this is very white.'" As those responses suggest, even the improving de-mographic measures of quality of life in Hartford and the seemingly dramatic increase in its racial diversity still have not made it as comfortable a place for its non-white residents as it has historically been for white residents.

This small window into the social, economic, and geographic inequalities within and across Upper Valley towns illuminates how this historical struc-ture underlies contemporary processes of racial inequality.

––––––

As this chapter has shown, the interactions between longtime white residents of the Upper Valley and the newer residents of color attempting to negotiate their role and right to belong in their chosen community have been affected both by the motivations and expectations of those newcomers and by shifts in the economies and demographics of the area. A closer look at the census data of specific towns across the region also reveals variations in the larger trends of racial diversification and social and economic disparities within core and peripheral communities that have meaningful implications for the ways in which newcomers of color have been received by the still predominantly white population and for their own sense of belonging to those communities. The following chapter moves beyond this structural analysis of the Upper Valley to examine the ways in which its cultural characteristics—the habits, values, dispositions, norms, and beliefs that guide behaviors—have also shaped the complex social relations between the old and new residents of the area.

TWO

A Cultural Portrait of the Upper Valley

When the town clerk of Stratton, Vermont, a small town west of the Upper Valley, found himself without a good image for the cover of the 2019–20 Town Report, he decided to use instead a widely distributed meme he had come across online:

> Welcome. You came here from there because you didn't like it there, and now you want to change here to be like there. We are not racist, phobic or anti whatever-you-are, we simply like here the way it is and most of us actually came here because it is not like there, wherever there was. You are welcome here, but please stop trying to make here like there. If you want here to be like there you should not have left there to come here, and you are invited to leave here and go back there at your earliest convenience.

This decision, like the alleged lynching attempt discussed in the previous chapter, prompted both local and national indignation on social media by responders who found the meme, despite its claims otherwise, not simply unwelcoming but xenophobic and racist. Both Stratton's location near a popular ski resort and the timing of the report's publication in early 2021 coincided with widespread and rising concerns within the region about rural gentrification in the wake of the pandemic.[1] The abashed clerk soon found it necessary to apologize to "anyone who was offended or affected by it. I didn't mean to get anyone upset. I just didn't think it through" (O'Connor 2021). His surprise at the response generated by the meme suggests that he had reason to believe that its sentiments would be widely shared within the community and merely reflected a commonsense view of local social expectations.[2] His choice thus seems to have unwittingly made explicit a set of assumed cultural norms and beliefs that may have served to forge a sense of social solidarity among longtime residents but also symbolically excluded new residents whose experiences and worldviews differed from the community's culturally normative landscape.[3]

As the demographic analysis in the previous chapter has shown, even though the Upper Valley has become increasingly racially diverse over the past few decades, its population, like that of much of Northern New England, is still overwhelmingly white. As a result, this chapter argues, the Upper Valley continues to function *culturally* as what Embrick and Moore (2020) have defined as a white space—a space in which the prevailing norms, beliefs, values, and logics of the community serve to uphold a social structure that creates social barriers for non-white people and that, as the rest of the book will show, makes it more difficult for them to create a sense of home for themselves in their new setting. To better understand the conscious and unconscious ways in which these processes operate, this chapter analyzes the survey responses of white residents and the interview responses of non-white residents collected by this study to uncover the cultural assumptions that shape the perceptions of and interactions among residents in their everyday settings. As that analysis reveals, three particular features of the area's culture present barriers to full inclusion and feelings of home for many non-white residents: a long-accepted norm of social reserve, a certain blindness toward the increasing racial diversity of the area and the impact of that blindness in the lives of people of color, and a general belief that it is the responsibility of newcomers to conform to the existing culture rather than the other way around. The chapter thus uncovers the cultural substrate on which the processes of misrecognition gain their energy and function to exclude people of color as full members of the Upper Valley community.

A Culture of Reserve

New Englanders have long been described and even caricaturized as reserved, self-reliant, and taciturn, particularly in their social relations with strangers. The stock dramatic figure of the shrewd, stubborn, and standoffish Yankee predates the American Revolution, and the apparent persistence of those characteristics is demonstrated by one historian's later description of the mythological New Englanders as "a people who chose to be pessimists rather than optimists, frugal not wasteful, introvert not extrovert" (Pierson 1955, 14). That this perception of the people of the region as private and reticent, often to the point of aloofness, is still widely held is evidenced by travelers' rating the New England states as among the "least friendly" in the nation in a 2019 survey (Big 7 Travel 2019). In a 2018 article, travel writer and former New England resident Joe Keohane described New Englanders as "stubborn, opinionated, aggressive, curt, contrary, distrustful, judgmental, irritable, and totally hilarious. (And warm and loyal, if you're willing to put in the work, though you can probably get a law degree in less time.) They view bluntness as an act of mercy and politeness as pointless nicety. Their interest in you is to be earned, not assumed."

Although, as Keohane pointed out, such reserve is not necessarily without its virtues, participants in this study agreed that the portrait of social relations in the area as generally chilly was largely accurate. When asked to identify any habits, customs, or ways of living within the Upper Valley that stood out in their minds as different from those of other places they had been, many white survey participants described the local culture as less warm or welcoming than those they had experienced elsewhere. One longtime resident, for example, commented, "I do think people in the South are much politer and kind. Recently spent time in Georgia. Very warmly greeted by everyone."[4] Another resident described this regional difference in more neutral terms, observing that "neighbors are cordial enough but value their privacy; they also respect mine. One cannot strike up a conversation with New Englanders as one might in the Midwest or South (where I have lived previously)." Seemingly echoing Upper Valley native Noah Kahan's claim in his 2022 hit song "Homesick" that "I'm mean because I grew up in New England," another survey participant admitted that people in other regions might see the public behavior of residents as rude: "When shopping in the Upper Valley, I notice that people aren't as polite. They don't say excuse me. They don't move in an aisle. And they don't smile when passing by." This reluctance to interact with people they do not know was also noted by several others, who observed that people in the area "tend to keep to themselves," "mind their own business," and "aren't as friendly" as people elsewhere in the country, a few going so far as to describe such behavior as "standoffishness" and people in the Upper Valley as "closed-minded, cold, and old!!"

Despite this seeming consensus, a number of the white residents who responded to the survey also described that impression of standoffishness as somewhat misleading. Some even described the culture of the area as warm, with the caveat that warmer forms of interaction may be reserved for one's close friends or for people willing to put time and effort into earning trust and membership within the community. One commenter, for instance, described people in their community not as cold or unkind but as "guarded" around people they did not know well and thus "inclined to keep to their small group of friends. Very different than Cleveland, Ohio, where I lived prior to moving here [and people were] much more social and welcoming of newcomers. Since moving here, I am guilty of only socializing with established circle of friends." Another very clearly articulated that friendly social relations tend to be limited to longtime Upper Valley residents, who are in turn "loyal to people who originated here." Others explained the seeming disjuncture between public and private behavior by making a distinction between overt friendliness and kindness, arguing that although Upper Valley residents may demonstrate little of the former, they practice plenty of the latter. Indeed, one resident who had lived in the area for almost thirty years described it as actually "much friendlier and courteous than most places I visit—though New England crabbiness can mask this." Another seemed to agree, noting that "people tend to keep to themselves but won't hesitate to help when asked." Another argued that the chilliness for which the area was well known was something that could thaw with effort and time: "Folks here hew to the New Englanders' way of living—not generally warm and friendly. Reserved. This 'reserve' took some adjustment. Warmth does surface—in time."

Many of the people of color I interviewed also described New England culture as more reserved than they had experienced in other parts of the country. According to Eswari, an Indian physician who had lived in her town only a year, the regional difference was prevalent enough that new residents seemed to have little choice but to adopt it themselves:

> In Arkansas, people were a lot more friendly, even though [we were] in a place where there were not many Indians at all. When we would go to McDonalds or any place like that, people always made an effort to make a conversation. They would be very curious and ask more about India. And we used to walk around the building and people would always acknowledge and say "Hi" or just exchange a conversation. I thought people were really nice. They would hold the door for you and all that. I did notice that here it is different. Even [at work], people don't look at you and don't say "Hi." I always used to wait until they looked at me so I could kind of smile, but I don't do that anymore. Now I don't even make an effort. I'm on my phone when I am in the hallway.

Another interviewee, Eunice, a Korean American woman, described most of the people she encountered in the area as highly regulating their emotions, resulting in social relations that she compared to the weather in the region: "Northern New England is a lot colder—its weather and its people. There is a norm that you should control your emotions carefully. You shouldn't be too loud, or laugh too much, or cry in public, or cry at all." Although these new residents recognized such regional differences as cultural preferences and habits of mind that long predated their own arrival in the region, some also described ways in which the results created particular social barriers for people of color. Eunice, for example, noted that the emotional regulation she observed among longtime residents often manifested itself as an aversion to conflict that, intentionally or not, served to create distance between white and non-white people: "The culture has norms about respectful equals not creating conflict, which means that you'll never have a substantive conversation about race. Ever." This and a number of similar responses from other interviewees echoed the findings of previous studies that people of color who engage in daily interaction with white people in such places as workplaces often feel pressured to downplay emotions such as anger or annoyance and to present a consistently pleasant demeanor not only to fit into prevailing norms but also to avoid conforming to negative racial stereotypes (e.g., Wingfield 2010).

People of color who came from communities where connection with one's neighbors was more prevalent and expected appeared to feel that this kind of emotional detachment and cultural emphasis on individual freedom was especially socially isolating. One such interviewee, Folade, a Nigerian woman who had lived in the Upper Valley for two years, reported that although she had hoped to develop close relationships with her neighbors, she had found that "individualism trumps community. It is very different in Nigerian culture. People check up on you. They just want to know how you are doing. They want to visit you. [Here,] I see my neighbors and I have to be the one to say 'Hi.'" Junior, who had immigrated to the United States to escape political repression in Haiti, also reported receiving a chilly reception in the community: "When you are walking down the street and you see someone, as you get closer, they try to distract themselves on their phone or something. We have survived it. Four years now. It's working. But on the human side—like, social relationships—it is a huge adjustment. What I am saying is I am open, but . . . they don't want to befriend people that are different, which is a loss." Camila, a middle-aged Afro-Latina woman who had lived in her town three years, assessed the culture this way: "People go about their daily lives, but they are cordial. Sometimes I feel like people are a little bit cold, but I don't know if it is because they are just having a rough day." Georgia, an older Black professional woman also relatively new to the area, observed the same coolness but claimed she had personally grown from the experience of adapting to it: "It is such a tight-knit community, you really have to put an effort out there to meet other people. I am very friendly, but I think moving here has made me even more outgoing because you have to speak up." Another middle-aged Black woman, Emma, who had lived in her town for eleven years, felt that this amount of time and experience in her community had given her insight into reasons for the coolness:

> I feel like it has taken me a long time to build community in comparison to other places I have lived. Here, the feeling is, especially among the locals, if your family has been here, you are more likely to be integrated into the community. And the culture is different. I feel like there is a New England sensibility to give boundaries, to give people space. I think this is actually a courtesy in some ways, but it could feel isolating to somebody who doesn't already have a community built in.

On the other hand, Ayana, a late-twenties Black woman who had lived in her town for just a year, noted the contrast between the greetings she received from white people and from people in the Black community:

> Let me tell you what happened. I was out with some friends and there was a Black man I had never seen before in my life walking down the sidewalk. He was walking the opposite way, but he turned and came back, and he was like, "Hey, I just wanted to come over here and say hello, and I am so happy to see you-all." And another time I went to the [small regional] airport and there was a Black woman there, and she came up to me and she said, "Oh my gosh, I have never seen you before. Please take down my number. Let me know if you need anything or how I can help you." It was like I was on *Survivor* or something.

Ayana's repeated experience of having Black people she did not know joyously reach out to her with offers of support seemed to suggest a shared desire for closer connection than that offered them by the cultural reserve of their new predominantly white community.

Overall, the survey and interview responses describe a broadly accepted culture of reserve in the Upper Valley marked by longtime residents' being less open to connection with people who are not already part of their established social circles and by a certain guardedness to social relations in both public and private settings. This underlying coolness results in a closed social environment in which newcomers, regardless of their race, tend to have a harder time settling in and feeling at home than in other places they have lived. As the next chapter will show, this culture of reserve enables misrecognition processes in which people of color feel unseen and unvalued, ultimately preserving the status quo of white cultural dominance even as the region diversifies.

A Culture of Colorblindness

During our interview, Saanvi, speaking of the predominantly white members of her community, reported, "They don't know me. They don't know I exist." An analysis of the survey and interview data collected by this study indicates that such feelings of invisibility among residents of color are largely a result of a broader culture of ignorance regarding the fact and impact of racial diversity that white residents frequently described as a neutral colorblindness. As previous scholars have argued and the responses of both my white and non-white participants seemed to support, however, professing not to "see color" ultimately serves to uphold the power and status of white people while protecting them from personal blame for obvious racial inequalities in society (Bonilla-Silva 2018; Mueller 2020).

To better understand the actual level of white residents' awareness of changes in the racial diversity of the Upper Valley, the opening question of my survey asked, "Over the past few decades, there has been an increase in the non-white population in the Upper Valley. Have you experienced this racial population change in your town?" Given the widespread and rapid demographic changes described in the previous chapter, I was surprised to find that a majority (59 percent) of the respondents answered "No" to this question. An analysis of the participants' responses to the follow-up question, "Please share your observations about racial and ethnic change that has taken place in your town," indicated that 10 percent of those who had answered the first question in the negative actually were aware of such changes, leading me to reclassify them as "Yes" answers. However, the results still indicate that nearly half of these white respondents reported being unaware of recent changes in the racial and ethnic makeup of their towns.[5]

Most of the follow-up comments of the participants who remained categorized as answering "No" to this question attributed their response either to their daily life being circumscribed in ways that prevented them from intersecting regularly with people of non-white descent or to the population of the Upper Valley still being so overwhelmingly white that (as one quipped) "this area is like wonder bread." As an examination of these follow-up comments revealed, a large number appeared to want to make clear that this response should not be viewed as intentionally exclusionary or racist. One respondent, for example, while acknowledging that "I do not have a lot of interaction with people that are non-white or immigrants," added that "this is not by choice." Another went so far as to express some regret about how "very little racial and ethnic change has occurred in this town. This is a white state—and this town may be one of the whitest. It is unfortunate (as I mentioned earlier) that we can't attract more racial diversity." A handful of others responded somewhat defensively to the question, asserting that they did not view things in terms of race; such answers included "does not concern me at all," "people are people to me," "we are all equal," and one respondent's claim to be "indifferent. I don't care who lives here regarding race or religion." A few respondents who answered "No" seemed to object to the very question, such as the resident who responded, "No, the next 9 questions are about race, not about change. Your survey is bullshit!!!" Another was less angry but still defensive in his objection: "I haven't even noticed. Honestly, it doesn't bother me. We're all equal, I could never be racist." These sentiments and seeming lack of cognizance of the actual racial diversification occurring around them may be explained by what geographer Yi-Fu Tuan refers to as *rootedness*, or the tendency of "long habitation of one locality" to lead residents of rural places to feel "at home in an unselfconscious way." Although, as Tuan points out, rootedness can have a positive valence, it also implies a "pastness" and stagnation, an inability or lack of desire to change and evolve, and an "incuriosity toward the world at large and an insensitivity toward the flow of time" (1980, 4).

Among the white respondents who did report having noticed changes in the racial makeup of their towns, many cited observing a shift in food options and an increase in ethnic restaurants, such as the person who remarked, "I see small restaurants and food booths at Summer Farmers Market featuring foods from varied cultures and staffed by people with features and accents from other cultures. I am glad for this and enjoy the foods, but I see less of the diversity in my daily life in my neighborhood." Another had noticed the presence of more non-white service workers: "I just recognize there is a continuing increase to Blacks and Indians and Chinese/Asians coming into [town]—restaurant workers, service people, etc." A number of respondents in this group appeared to assume that the racial changes they had observed were the result of local labor shortages, such as one who responded that "we have a shortage of workers. Some employers have brought 'ethnic' workers to fill the need." That the respondents who expressed an awareness of racial change in their communities had noticed that shift primarily in the low-wage, service sector rather than among the professional migrants who actually constitute the vast majority of the racialized minority population in the Upper Valley suggests a general misperception among longtime white residents of the actual demographics and contributions of their new fellow residents.

Although most of the survey participants who described recent racial changes in their towns did so in largely positive or neutral terms, a minority explicitly expressed some negative judgments or concerns about what those changes might mean for their communities. Among those few, some worried about increased drug activity, such as one who claimed to have observed "an increase of young black men that seem to be bringing in the drugs into this town with out-of-state plates." Another respondent expressed a concern that the arrival of such in-migrants could lead to an increase in "violent crime" and "dominating aggression," a worry about the future that appears to reflect stereotypical notions of immigrant criminality and the spatial stigmas, or negative perceptions of particular locales, that often accompany people of color moving from urban areas.[6] Similarly, another respondent, while claiming to be fine with the growing number of people of color in the area, nonetheless appeared to associate it with drug activity: "I don't mind different races coming to town but do know that NJ, NY, and MA folks are coming into town to deliver drugs—not okay in that instance." Even among the respondents who expressed some worries about this demographic shift, a number also appeared eager to avoid appearing discriminatory or racist, such as one who appeared to associate these changes with an increase in "racial politics" but to also want to disassociate herself from that term's negative connotations: "I do see more POCs in town now, more frequently than before, and I see more racial politics going on in the area too. I have no issues with this personally." Still other respondents framed their negative responses to these demographic changes not in explicit racial terms but as a sense of loss of community or continuity, such as one who observed, "We have lost a lot of 'old home' feeling. Due to College and [hospital] importing to fill jobs. Residents don't seem to come for a lifetime!!" Although this response accurately reflects that many of the members of racial and ethnic minorities who have moved to the region have done so to take professional jobs, it also seems to also dehumanize and objectify those newcomers as imported and presumably temporary goods, rather than as individuals with valuable skills and choices about where they live who are equally invested in developing and sustaining a sense of home in the Upper Valley.

Despite most of the white respondents' claims that they were either largely unaware or generally accepting of the growing racial diversity of the region, many of the people of color I interviewed perceived this supposed colorblindness less as a lack of racism than as an active ignorance regarding their own

experiences living in this predominantly white space. A number of those interviewees reported being particularly disappointed that many of their white
friends and colleagues, most of whom considered themselves politically progressive, appeared incapable of grasping the extent to which they regularly experienced being singled out or excluded in ways they saw as racist. One such
respondent was Eunice, who described being saddened by the inability of her
white friends, and even her white husband, to fully appreciate what it felt like
to be a person of color in a majority white space, such as the time she attended
a sporting event with a group of her white peers:

> I said, "It is such a relief to see like a dozen other adults of color in these
> bleachers." One of my friends said to me, "Oh, that's ridiculous. We are
> all just human anyway and race doesn't mean anything. So, to count the
> number of POCs here is just ridiculous." The other friend of mine who
> was sitting next to her said, "Oh gosh, that's a really good point." Mean
> while, my husband is tapping me on the leg, saying, basically, "Please
> don't get into it, please just let it go." So, I had to deal with (a) Ignoramus
> Number One, who would say something like that, and (b) the collusion
> of the other person who isn't even smart enough to say, "Whoa, did you
> just say that?" And then there was the collusion of my own white spouse!
> He was basically telling me, "I know exactly what you're thinking. I com
> pletely agree that that is literally the craziest thing to ever say, but please
> don't cause any conflict."

Despite her disappointment at what she saw as a lack of understanding and
support among some of her closest allies, Eunice wanted to make clear that
she saw this ignorance of the lived experiences of residents of color as a broader
cultural phenomenon in the area: "White people assume that it is just a misunderstanding. I don't think most white people in the Upper Valley have any idea
how much unearned comfort or safety [they have]. Especially when people say
things like, 'You know, we just live in the most perfect place.' And I'm like,
perfect for whom?"

Another interviewee, Steven, shared another example of the seemingly
widespread belief among white residents that racism is not a problem in the
Upper Valley:

Here's a great example of it where I just, oof. I was at a dinner party, and [a white man] said to me, "Are you thrilled to be in New England?" And I said, "What do you mean by that?" And he says, "Well, you know, the South is so backwards and racist, and this is such a progressive liberal area. I would just think that, as a Black person, you would love to be here." And I said, "Interesting. I would love to hear the data you have to inform that perspective. So, give me the names of Black people you have talked with to inform you that this is a healthy and wholesome place for Black people to live." He couldn't give me a single person. He couldn't call a friend. He just had no reference point. But that perspective is indicative of how I daily interact with people. That kind of assumption is what I do not like about this area. It's unacknowledged. For some reason they think that they have enough degrees where they have educated themselves away from the racism. The Upper Valley postures itself as having the right pedigree, they know all the right things to say.

After sharing other examples of such colorblindness among white, educated, progressive residents of the Upper Valley, including his own friends and colleagues, Steven went on to explain how such experiences contributed to a larger sense of unease and uncertainty about his standing in the community:

But I mean this wholeheartedly, I never truly understand where I stand with people. And that is something I never experience in the South. I know where I stand with people, by what you say or what you drive. But in New England, there is an arrogance of superiority and that rarely happens in the South. I think everyone, particularly in this community, they know what to say. They know how to vote. They know the terminology to use. But I just truly never know what they think about me. It could be a dear colleague, but how do they really feel about me? I don't know. Are they truly in for me? Or are they gunning for me? I just never know. That is something I think about a lot, and it is very unsettling.

This kind of unease expressed by a number of newcomers of color seemed due in large part to a disappointed expectation that politically progressive residents and colleagues would be more aware of the meaning and impacts of racial inequality. Indeed, Ayana reported that moving to the Upper Valley had opened her eyes to the ubiquity of racism even among left-leaning people:

I typically go out running around my community, and I run past homes and different businesses that still, even [three years] after the [2016] election, have Trump signs outside. But I also see businesses and houses that have quotes from Dr. Martin Luther King and Black Lives Matter. What I'm learning here is, whether you identify as Democrat or Republican, it doesn't necessarily define how you view people of color. Because I have met [people] from both parties that are racist and that have said some pretty derogatory terms regarding people of color. That's definitely one thing that I have always known, but it really kind of opened my eyes a little bit after moving.

Georgia reported observing a similar lack of awareness among white people even in a space in which she thought she had reason to expect more racial sensitivity on the part of her colleagues, a workforce diversity training session:

A lady commented that racism doesn't exist in the Upper Valley. And someone else chimed in and agreed. And then someone else said they didn't know what they could do to help because racism isn't an issue here in the Upper Valley. You know, I just kept hearing it. I [told myself] that day I wasn't going to be the person who speaks up. There were about seventy of us, and I think there were only maybe four minorities. I can remember the lady who said it, but I don't hold it against her. I think she said it from a good place, and she was saying that her daughter does all this volunteer work to help educate. I don't take a lot of things too personal, but it was irritating me that they kept saying, "Oh no, we don't have those issues here, and we don't have that, we don't experience that here." You know, people are genuinely good, but you do have some bad apples.

These stories speak not only to the prevalence of seemingly willful ignorance of racial inequality even among highly educated and progressive people regarding the experiences of their non-white neighbors, friends, and colleagues but also to the emotional costs of that ignorance for people of color who regularly confront situations that require them to calculate whether a response, be it expressing irritation or educating others, is likely to be a worthwhile use of their energy.

Although some sense of cultural distance between residents from different backgrounds is probably inevitable, the interviewees almost universally concluded that this distance was exacerbated by the reluctance of longtime residents, despite the normative white liberalism of the community, to openly discuss matters of racial and cultural difference. This informal and supposedly colorblind "don't ask, don't tell" policy was disconcerting to those interviewees, who experienced it as a form of silencing that did not allow them to fully be themselves. Eunice was clear about how others' not valuing her experiences of racial difference or not taking them seriously enough to be worthy of discussion made her feel distant from many in the community:

> I do not think most people in the Upper Valley value the experiences of people of color. I don't think they even validate what we endure by living here. One of the reasons why I say that is people aren't even willing to acknowledge that race is an issue. A lot of white liberals think that as long as race never comes up as an issue, it doesn't exist in the Upper Valley. People who are liberal often make it impossible for their friends who are people of color to mention race. They do not signal any openness to talking about or acknowledging race. You don't have to interrogate people, but there are people I talk to openly about my experiences and then there are people that I will never, ever say anything to them because they are not trustworthy. And the thing I would like white people in the Upper Valley to know is that if you have a person of color in your life and they have never talked to you about race, that's saying something about you and how safe those people feel talking to you.

According to Eunice, there appeared to be only one manner in which white people in her community were willing to engage with the subject of race:

> People will bring up race as a news topic. They have some things to say about what they read in the *New York Times* or the *New Yorker*. They will gasp, "This is horrible! I can't believe that!" But if race comes up as it relates to something that happened to me, much of the time I get gaslighted. I get told, "That didn't really happen. That couldn't have happened. Are you sure that happened? I'm sure that didn't have anything to do with race."

Eunice's experiences and theories illustrate how a culture of white liberalism can prevent open acknowledgment of the individual, human dimension of racialized encounters and how the lengths to which many white people go to preserve their sense of good character can end up pushing people of color away, as they do not feel fully seen when their experiences are discounted.

Eunice's observations about white unwillingness to acknowledge the racialized underpinnings of social encounters within the Upper Valley were also affirmed by Saima and Emma during their interviews. Saima reported being particularly disappointed by the responses of white friends and colleagues when she would try to explain the subtle racial nature of an encounter: "I have shared some of these experiences as teaching moments, because I want to share things that they maybe should not do, or how their good intentions are not enough. With white people, it's always defensive. It's always like, 'Oh. But I think they meant this.' What I find is that people always want to make excuses for racist behavior. [They say] that I should be forgiving." Sharing Saima's deduction that such responses demonstrated attempts by white people to distance themselves from guilt and responsibility for such occurrences, Emma attributed many white residents' shock and awkward responses to racist incidents to a similarly self-protective form of denial:

> I am amazed by how surprised people are that this happens within their community. But that is not comforting. It is just unnerving. I feel like, I am telling you something and you should believe me right off the bat. I think they are in denial. They want to believe that they live in such a wonderfully progressive community and that it wouldn't happen here. I'm like, it happens all the time! I would like if I got some more information back from them, like "I find this upsetting. Can you tell me more?" But I guess when we are surprised, we fight, flight, or freeze. And they are in that moment, where this information is disarming to them, and they literally freeze.

While Emma explains the denial away as a natural human response to threat, she and Saima also suggest that some conscious effort on the part of white people to respond thoughtfully and without defensiveness might go a long way to reassure the people of color in their lives that they are heard, valued, trusted, and safe discussing their experiences with racism.

Overall, the picture painted by the survey and interview responses is one of a climate in which a lack of understanding about racial change and the reality and impact of racism is not merely practiced by a few isolated individuals but a cultural norm that saturates the Upper Valley community. Yet as the experiences of people of color disclosed in the following chapters suggest, this seemingly willful colorblindness is also ultimately self-serving. As this book argues, such colorblindness should be viewed not simply as an innocent or unwitting absence of knowledge among white people but as a core process that serves to uphold white domination and privilege, a form of white ignorance that Mueller (2020) describes as serving as an "ends-based technology" of white supremacy. The resulting cultural context allows white people of all classes to maintain their dominant social status and resources and to do so relatively guilt-free, even as it creates an environment that makes it difficult for people of color to fully consider the Upper Valley home.

A Culture of Assimilation

An analysis of the responses of the white respondents to the final set of questions of the survey further reveals that the attitudes expressed by the meme on the cover of the Stratton town report reflect not merely a specific regional context or historical moment but a larger ideology of assimilation that has long been central to the cultural fabric of the Upper Valley and the United States more broadly.[7] The behavioral expectations promoted by this assimilationist ideology were perhaps articulated most clearly in response to the migration of large numbers of presumably "ethnic" Southern, Central, and Eastern Europeans to the country in search of greater labor opportunities at the turn of the twentieth century. The relative speed and ease with which many of those immigrants and their children appeared to adopt the racial identity of the white majority (albeit aided by their shared European heritage, progressive-era social programs, and later economic expansion following World War II) served to bolster the conventional wisdom that the best way to get ahead in American society was to adopt the values, behaviors, and culture of the majority. As numerous critical scholars have observed, however, this ideology serves to leave the beliefs and practices of the dominant white culture uninterrogated and to unfairly place the burden of change on society's newcomers.

To better understand the impact that this belief system may have had on the expectations and behaviors of longtime white residents in the Upper

Valley, the survey asked the following fixed-response question: "Some people argue that newcomers should adopt the local culture when they move to a new place. Others argue that newcomers should be free to live according to their own customs. Which of these is closer to your views?" That question was then followed by an open-ended one asking respondents to explain the reasons behind their choice. Although these questions did not mention race specifically, the previous questions had identified these "newcomers" as non-white and the context as racial and ethnic change within the respondents' towns. Together, these questions were intended to help uncover ways in which the culture of the Upper Valley, without necessarily being explicitly or consciously racist, may function to maintain white residents' position at the top of the racial hierarchy and perpetuate racial inequality by privileging the status quo.

As might perhaps be expected given the white survey participants' eagerness to disassociate themselves from possible accusations of racism in their responses to the previous questions, only slightly more than a fifth (21 percent) explicitly agreed with first question's statement that newcomers should expect to adopt the local culture.[8] As an analysis of the follow-up write-in responses revealed, however, 29 percent of the respondents who disagreed with that statement in their first answer nonetheless went on to explain that choice in ways that stipulated some limits to newcomers' free expression of their own cultural practices. Taken together, therefore, the responses to this final set of questions indicated that a full half of the white survey participants believed that newcomers should be expected to limit their cultural expression.

Although some of the participants who initially agreed that "newcomers should adopt the local culture when they move to a new place" chose not to take the opportunity to explain their reasoning, an analysis of the responses of those who did revealed that more than two thirds (69 percent) fell into one or more of three assimilationist behavioral expectations: that newcomers to the Upper Valley should (1) be willing to change their own culture, (2) not expect to change the existing white-dominated culture of the area, and (3) follow the existing norms and customs of their new communities. As the following discussion of each of these sentiments demonstrates, each functioned as an interrelated and mutually reinforcing aspect of a coherent and powerful cultural belief system that devalues the cultures of people "not from around here," deems them unworthy of inclusion into the community as they are, and tasks them with the social burden of ensuring that longtime residents are not made to feel uncomfortable.

Change Your Culture

Of those responses that indicated that newcomers should expect to make at least some concessions to the predominant culture of the region, about a quarter directly stated that residents should be prepared to change their own cultures if they hope to access the rights and privileges of belonging. Among those, a few expressed that expectation as an obligatory directive or demand, including one respondent who appeared to bluntly invoke a nationalist stance: "This is our town and country. We do not adjust, they should." The hard logic of this respondent's division of people into categories of "our/we" and "they" at both the local and national level communicated his belief in strict and exclusive group boundaries. By stating this expectation in the form of a common expression, another respondent seemed to frame it as simply a commonsense suggestion: "When in Rome. It keeps people who are set in their ways (most of us) comfortable and not so angry about newcomers." Despite her less demanding and exclusionary tone, this respondent nonetheless implied that the newcomers of color in her community were essentially sojourners in a foreign space and assigned them responsibility for making sure the predominantly white locals can continue to feel secure in their dominant social status. A third resident justified an assimilationist response by invoking a seemingly universal democratic principle, claiming that "if you move to an area you should adapt, not think it adapts to you. It's called majority rule." Even though most Americans are likely to agree in principle with this tenet of democracy, such demands can produce an unequal outcome that, as the following chapters will make clear, ultimately oppresses newcomers by denying their individual rights of expression within the collective.

The remaining responses that fell into this category promoted the same goal, following a softer logic by which newcomers were advised to assimilate to the local culture for their own good, a position that has been termed *benevolent assimilation* (Ngai 2004). One such respondent harkened back to a now largely discredited trope of the American project as a melting pot to suggest that the only way for newcomers to become fully accepted is to blend into the area's already established culture: "Without some degree of assimilation, the melting of cultures does not happen, and newcomers are considered 'others' instead of community members or neighbors." Another respondent framed assimilationist rhetoric as an appeal to human nature and a compassionate concern for newcomers' well-being: "If you don't adopt at least some of the local customs you will have a hard time living in an area. People, being social creatures, find a level of contentedness in fitting in." Another resident expressed similar advice in the form of a warning that newcomers of color are likely to risk social ostracism and negative assessments of their character unless they find a way to fit into the dominant ways of being: "If they fail to consider the existing patterns and customs, they are missing something and are essentially anti-social." This segment of respondents thus framed their claims more softly, arguing for assimilation using language that implied newcomers would be better off—happier, accepted, social—if they tried to fit in.

As the experiences of people of color analyzed in the following chapters demonstrate, such expectations that newcomers should be willing to change their behavior to assimilate into their new communities, whether stated as obligatory or benevolent, place the burden on them to fit into the dominant cultural mold if they hope to feel at home. In this sense, assimilation is not simply a process of "becoming similar" but a negotiation of power with a dominant group that reserves the right to define deservingness according to their own standards.

Don't Change Our Culture

Of the respondents who expressed assimilationist views, more than a third focused on how newcomers should regard the existing culture of the Upper Valley rather than how they should maintain their own cultures. The prevailing sentiment articulated by these comments closely mirrored that of the meme used on the Stratton Town Report: newcomers should not aspire to change the way things have always been done in their new communities. This set of responses thus appeared to reflect the survey participants' desire to maintain what Blumer (1958) has described as the white population's "proprietary advantage" in setting the standards for good and proper behavior and to imply that people of color have a responsibility to perform their racial identities in non-threatening ways.

Although almost half of the responses that fell in this category were expressed as friendly and broadly applicable advice, their actual wording often revealed an underlying feeling of being under threat, such as that of one white respondent who urged in-migrants to "allow local customs to proceed without being insulted, like holidays as they have been celebrated for many years. Try to assimilate and not force your new location to change to your ways." Such sentiments seemed to reflect some anxiety among white respondents that the full inclusion of racial and ethnic minorities in their cultural landscape could threaten their own singular ability to define cultural norms, expressed as fears that racial and ethnic minorities might "try to change me" or "implement their own customs as 'be all.'" That none of those respondents reported any actual efforts to change cherished local customs seemed to suggest that their fears were based primarily on potential loss of their own cultural hegemony and perhaps derived from a larger national political discourse and rhetoric. Such anxieties appeared to underlie even the responses of those who posed their suggestions to newcomers in terms of respect and tolerance, such as the resident who stated, "I would prefer they share their ideas and beliefs but not take away from the culture of everyone else. Everyone should respect everyone, and sharing should be done in an open-minded and non-threatening way." This respondent's underlying assumption that newcomers who might choose to continue to practice or to seek public recognition of their own customs would somehow "take away from" or "threaten" the "culture of everyone else" seemed to reflect a somewhat broader apprehension among white residents that the cultural calculus of the region represented a zero-sum game in which their own automatic claims to belonging in the Upper Valley were jeopardized by the inclusion of racialized minorities.

A few of these responses seemed to go yet a step further in this direction, implying that acknowledging and honoring other cultural traditions would somehow diminish what was most civilized, good, and prized about these communities and by so doing represent a possible threat to social order. This set of responses implied a sense of cultural superiority in language that at times again seemed to echo the cover of the Stratton Town Report, such as "people should move here because they like what it is now" and "it's nice here now, why change it?" Another resident seemed to imply that any efforts by newcomers to change things would be somehow nondemocratic, stating that newcomers should "not infringe on the rights/practices of those in the community." Another responded, "I don't care as long as they don't try to impede or change local cultures or try to impose theirs on us," while yet another stipulated that newcomers should be allowed to "keep their customs as long as they are not disruptive to others." These respondents' use of words such as *infringe, impede, impose,* and *disrupt* strongly implied that any attempt to change the cultural status quo would necessarily represent an unwanted threat or loss rather than a possible addition or improvement. Even though some of these respondents had initially stated that racial and ethnic minorities should be "free" to keep their customs, they did so only with the caveat that those practices must not rock the existing boat.

Overall, these participants' responses suggested that if newcomers of color want to become accepted as full members of the community, they must take care not to be seen as disregarding white freedoms, which in this case appeared to be the freedom to set cultural norms and expectations.[9] By declaring that newcomers should not "change our culture," these respondents seemed to argue from a position of group threat, articulating a desire to preserve the traditional white culture of the region that appeared to be based both on its inherent superiority and on a supposedly broadly shared preference for order and comfort. Such findings may also reflect some anticipatory anxiety among white residents that their freedom of expression could be hamstrung if other racial groups are also able to freely express themselves.

Follow the Rules

Another quarter or so of the white survey participants who expressed assimilationist views based them on a third behavioral expectation: new residents hoping to assimilate into the community should expect to follow the informal norms and formal laws that together constitute the time-honored "rules" established by the predominantly white population. Some of these responses framed their argument for the importance of following such rules in terms of shared personal and community values. In a particularly straightforward statement of the personal nature of such values, one respondent answered, "I don't care what nationality they are as long as they share the same values as me," while another similarly answered, "To each their own. I think as long as they abide with my views, I would be fine." A third respondent shifted the focus from herself to the larger community by saying she would accept new-comers if "they have the same values as our other neighbors," thereby high-lighting the importance of keeping things the way they are for the presumed good of the community. Another participant drew the connection between personal and community values and normative behaviors more explicitly, if also more locally specific and colloquially: "So long as they are a good neigh-bor who doesn't feed the turkeys." Such statements, while reflecting a desire among white residents to control the behaviors of newcomers so as to promote conformity and preserve their own comfort, also appeared to start from the premises that newcomers' beliefs and values are essentially different from those of long-term white residents and that their social acceptance therefore hinges on adopting what those residents define as "proper" behavior and "good" character. A few respondents specifically expressed a desire that newcomers should care about and invest in the future of the community, one responding that newcomers should "contribute to work in progress" and another that they would be welcome "as long as they are contributing members of society and send their kids to school." Such responses appeared to suggest that belonging to the community depends not only upon aligning one's personal values with those of existing residents but demonstrating a shared investment in the public good.

Some responses that fell in this category expanded the responsibility to honor current residents' personal and community values to include also ad-hering to a broader set of American values and practices. One resident, for ex-ample, briefly and emphatically identified several practices that he viewed as essential to demonstrating an adherence to such American values: "We have let them here, therefore, English main language, flag the only one!!" A number of other respondents who similarly advised in-migrants to demonstrate Ameri-can values also specifically mentioned the importance of speaking English, and as others have noted, a nation's flag and official language often serve as symbols of its history and the basis of a shared identity in diverse countries such as the United States (Kymlicka 1995). Yet the above-mentioned respondent's strong assertion that "we have let them here" also demonstrates what appears to be a sense of entitlement among some white English-speaking people based on what they view as an exclusive claim to a shared American history of hard work and sacrifice. These reactions to a failure to speak English or to honor the flag may reflect some long-standing residents' resentment toward newcomers of color whom they see as threatening to change or challenge important American values and as those are expressed at the local level.[10]

Yet another set of survey participants who suggested that newcomers should "follow the rules" defined those rules in terms of American legal rights and responsibilities. For example, one such respondent noted, "We still have laws and morals that define us as a nation" and all citizens should be expected to follow them, while another used similar terms to suggest that newcomers would be welcomed if they "value our legal system, understand and value our constitutional republic."[11] Another respondent, viewing the notion of "rules" in an explicitly legalistic sense, took issue with the wording of the survey question, which referred to customs and culture but did not specifically include the legal system: "Customs alone do not define a culture! As long as the custom is legal under U.S. LAW. However, they should participate in paying taxes and if permitted by their religion, they should vote." The respondent's use of punctuation and capitalization for emphasis and focus on paying taxes and voting demonstrates a strong belief that such civic responsibilities function as vital criteria for acceptance in these communities.

Several other participants seemed to support the notion of individual liberties but tempered their belief in personal autonomy by imposing limits, as in the parenthetical additions in the responses that residents "should be free (within reason)" and "live and let live (as long as it is safe)." Another respondent's two-part response indicated the belief that individuals' freedom to practice their culture depends on adherence to immigration law: "As long as people enter our country through the correct means, they should be able to live in any community." Yet another similarly expressed a strong belief in individual freedom while arguing it must also be bound by legal limits: "It is no one's business how we conduct our personal/private lives. We're all Americans as long as everyone recognizes and abides by rule of Law and Constitutional Guarantees." This respondent's assertion that the US Constitution properly serves as the ideological blueprint for freedom appears consistent with nationalistic rhetoric that holds that the public good depends upon "ordered liberty," in which the conflicting demands of personal freedom and public order are reconciled through individual self-control (Schwarzwalder 2014).

Overall, the survey responses reflect a widespread belief among white residents that newcomers to the Upper Valley should assimilate to local cultural expectations if they wish to be comfortable and accepted in their chosen community. In a variety of ways, those responses indicate that the social pressure toward cultural conformity is motivated not simply to smooth the path toward belonging for newcomers but also to preserve feelings of ease and security for longtime residents. The resulting expectation that newcomers bear the responsibility for change leaves the dominant culture of the area largely undisturbed, and with it a racial status hierarchy in which whiteness continues to rule.

————

Despite the economic and social differences among the small towns of the Upper Valley described in the previous chapter, the responses of both the white survey participants and the racialized minority interviewees from across the region reveal some strikingly consistent cultural behaviors and norms in the area. As this analysis of those data has shown, the interactions between old-timers and newcomers to the region are marked by a culture of reserve, colorblindness, and assimilation that together serve to maintain the status hierarchy from which longtime white residents benefit and to place the burden of fitting in on their newer neighbors of color, despite their actual economic, professional, and social contributions to their communities. The following chapter delves more deeply into the interview data collected from residents of color in an attempt to identify the particular mechanisms through which those cultural elements enable misrecognition and reproduce racial inequality in this rural setting.

THREE

How Misrecognition Works

In May 2020, Chris Brown set out from his home in Hartford, Vermont, to look for a Mother's Day gift. He hadn't gone far—just to the end of his road—when he was flagged down by two white men standing in front of their pickup truck. Brown stopped, rolled down his window to see if they needed help, and was confronted by one of the men, who, he reported, "just starts yelling at me, saying, 'You don't belong here. You know, we can't have people like you here.'" The man's next declaration—"We don't want your drugs and your crime and your COVID" (Merriman 2020)—clarified the reason Brown had been targeted for harassment: preconceptions about "people like you" and how they might threaten the community. Brown was able to verbally de-escalate the situation but decided to forgo the shopping trip and return home, as the interaction had left him very aware that some residents deemed him threatening and therefore unwelcome in his small town in rural Vermont.

The timing matters here. Spring 2020 was a time of national social upheaval and racial turmoil, heightened by social divisions about how to carry on under the threat of a novel and little-understood infectious disease. The national racial awakening associated with the murder of George Floyd later in May had been partially set in motion three months earlier by the vigilante killing of a young Black man, Ahmaud Arbery, by two white men in Georgia who saw him as "out of place" jogging in their neighborhood. Despite the chilling similarities between the situations in which Arbery and Chris Brown found themselves, the latter must also be understood in terms of the rural gentrification that had intensified across rural Northern New England during that period. The menacing situation that Chris Brown—a professor at a prestigious university in New York City who had moved with his family to their second home in Vermont during the pandemic—encountered that morning occurred not only because of his race but also because of his affluence and urbanicity. Though I did not interview Chris Brown for this study, he is an excellent representative of the type of people I did: professional people of color who had recently moved to the Upper Valley from an urban area. Although it is impossible to know whether the two white men who accosted Brown were aware of his actual identity, they would be far from the only residents of the area who found their rural sense of community and small-town way of life threatened by the city culture he represented, and their homes and economic livelihoods threatened by the rural gentrification they were beginning to see all around them. The unique class and racial structure of the Upper Valley thus set the stage for a complex and multifaceted culture clash.

Indeed, the residents of color interviewed for this study reported encountering multiple forms of *misrecognition*, defined here as the process of making cultural distinctions about certain groups of people as less valuable and worthy than others, as people whose feelings, opinions, and presence do not matter. In contrast to humans' universal desire for *recognition*, the term social scientists use for having one's vision of oneself as a good and valuable person reflected in others' reactions, misrecognition operates to draw social boundaries and maintain social hierarchies between people.[1] Such misrecognition can take a variety of forms and levels of overtness, from the kind of explicit and confrontational incident experienced by Chris Brown to more subtle and indirect forms that leave the recipients like Saanvi (the physician from India described in the introduction) wondering just where they stand in the community. Together, these forms of misrecognition constitute a major way in which dominant groups define social boundaries to exclude members of stigmatized groups and defend their own status as morally deserving of opportunities and resources. This chapter examines a number of complex and often painful interactions that interviewees reported having had with the predominantly white members of the small-town communities that made them feel like what Georg Simmel's classic work on social distance (1908) describes as "strangers"—as people who live "among the group" but are not "of the group." As the following analysis reveals, the misrecognition experienced by these newcomers of color operated through three main mechanisms: explicit racism, social distance, and provisional acceptance.

Explicit Racism

Despite the area's liberal reputation and the white survey participants' nearly universal denial of holding racist attitudes, many of my interviewees of color reported experiences of misrecognition that they viewed as openly racist. Ayana, a Black woman in her early twenties who had grown up in the South and moved to the Upper Valley for a professional job in fundraising, admitted that, despite loving her work and "being in new environments and meeting new people," she sometimes wished her job "would be uprooted and placed in a completely different area." As she explained, outside of the support she received from other people of color in an employee resource group she had joined, she had often felt very left out and actively excluded from her community:

> I really feel like my saving grace and my support system has been the people at [work], to be completely honest with you. I'm really, really thankful for them. Whatever the opposite of home is, that's how I would feel [without them]. It would feel very foreign to me. I wouldn't feel a sense of belonging at all. Not even that it wouldn't be a welcoming community to me, it would be a community that is actively trying to push me out. It's one of those things too, like I have experienced racism in other places. It's just never been so overt as I have seen it here. How comfortable people are in their words and in their actions, that has surprised me. I'm used to like a sprinkle of discrimination, and this is like a faucet just gushing out at you.

Asked for more details about what that steady stream of discrimination had entailed, Ayana described an explicitly racist encounter with an employee at a local Burger King:

> They asked me to pull to the front because [the meal] would take a second to cook. So, I pulled up, and they came outside and gave me the bag. I

checked the bag and was like, "Oh, you forgot the sauce. Do you mind if I have the sauce?" I had paid for it. It was on my receipt. He just rolled his eyes, and he was like, "I've got stuff to do. I have burgers to cook." And I was like, "I completely understand. You're busy. Just, would you mind grabbing the sauce for me?" It was in the midst of the pandemic, so I was not able to go into the restaurant and grab it myself. He goes inside and I thought that he was going to get it. So, I was just waiting patiently. And then he came out and he waved his hand, and [said], "N***r, move on."

Despite, or perhaps because of, the obviously racist and hostile intent behind the employee's actions and words that day, Ayana made the calculation to quietly accept the white worker's treatment and simply drive off: "I was like, this can go in two different ways. I can try to be combative. But, at the end of the day, I had to remind myself of where I was. And I'm like, I'm in the Upper Valley. I heard about these stories, but I hadn't experienced anything myself just yet. So, I was like, okay, I was warned. It is what it is." Although this rationalization allowed Ayana to protect her own self-image by externalizing the blame for her racist treatment to the structure and culture of the Upper Valley, it could not shield her from feelings of exclusion or the emotional labor of having to ponder how to best respond.

Even people of color who had lived in the Upper Valley for more than a decade reported still encountering explicit racism in service establishments. Fu, a Chinese man with a professional degree who worked at a medical software company, recalled a time his family had been openly berated because of their accent when ordering at a local restaurant:

There was one experience when we stopped to get lunch. It was a very small restaurant, and it was right in the middle of the rush hour. We were looking at the menu on the wall and trying to decide. The owner of the restaurant got impatient. When we ordered, she said, "I don't understand you. I don't understand you." I think my English was understandable. But then she said, "Okay, I'm not going to serve you anything. Just get out."

Though Fu and his family had lived in that town for eleven years by then and felt themselves part of the professional and social spaces of the area, their accents had triggered a xenophobic and intolerant response that served as a potent reminder of their outsider status.

That such explicit racism still operates as a mechanism for establishing social boundaries even at this point in time and in a region without a widely acknowledged history of institutionalized racism may be a function of the previously discussed socioeconomic inequality in the Upper Valley. The education and healthcare economies in which many of the newcomers of color interviewed for this study were employed also depend upon a large pool of employees and workers within the larger community who cannot afford to live in the core towns but commute from peripheral towns to work in service positions to support the dominant and growing professional class. In the incidents reported by Ayana and Fu, workers in such low-paid service positions appeared to draw upon the cultural tool kit available to them as longtime white residents to strengthen a boundary between *them* (in this case, residents of color they still view as outsiders in the Upper Valley) and *us* (white people who, despite their lower socioeconomic status, strongly believe in their own right to be there). Although such residents may not be in direct competition with professional people of color for jobs, explicit racism provides them a mechanism for maintaining what they view as their rightful position within the social and racial hierarchy of the area.

Such inter-class status competition did not appear to be the sole inspiration or motivation behind the incidents of explicit racism reported by this study's interviewees of color. A number of those interviewees, for instance, described racist encounters with longtime residents that they ascribed to stereotypes based on a lack of familiarity and experience with people of color. Samuel, a Haitian man who, after living in his town for fifteen years, claimed to generally feel well-integrated into the community, told a story of being summarily dismissed when he tried to ask a white woman he had just met out on a date:

> I went to Circle K over there by the bridge and there was this Caucasian lady. She was very talkative. That was my first time seeing her. And she was talking in a very pleasant, very friendly way. And then as she left, I say [to myself], "Maybe I need to go back and ask her for her number." And I follow my idea, and went right outside. As she was getting in her car, I said, "Hey young lady, maybe you don't mind give me your phone number?" She said, "Oh no, honey. I'm sorry. I don't do Black men." Yes! And I shake her hand [and] said, "Thank you very much. I really appreciate that." Be-

cause she would've taken me through a wild goose chase, knowing what she knows.

Even if Samuel may have been a bit too enthusiastic in approaching the woman for her phone number after engaging in just a brief conversation, her direct, negative response appeared to serve its intended purpose: to immediately shut down his overture. But although Samuel clearly understood that, to her, his identity as a Black man made taking the relationship beyond casual conversation a nonstarter, he seemed reluctant to attribute her categorical judgment of him to racism:

> It wasn't meant to insult me. I don't think so. It wasn't meant to demean me. There was a point she was making, and I need to accept that fact. But what do you say to that? How do you come back at that one? Other than accept, agree, shake hands, and bow out. Bow out very honestly and very proudly. Because I was proud when I turned around. Here I am in a white community. So, it is what it is. Some of them, they don't go there. And that's their right.

Samuel's choosing to attribute the woman's response to personal preference rather than to stereotypes that systematically mark Black men as unworthy companions is emblematic of the emotional labor that stigmatized individuals often learn to perform to ward off hurt feelings or personal responsibility for the negative treatment they receive.[2]

In addition to such encounters with strangers in public, some of the interviewees reported that their children had experienced explicit racism from their acquaintances at school. According to Eunice, a Korean American woman who had lived in her town for sixteen years, not even her kids' wealthy peers were shy about using explicitly racist language: "I haven't even talked about my kids! Like my son being called a C***k at school. It's one thing for me to be called a C***k in 1974, but I mean, this is 2019 in a liberal town! One of my friends is a white person who kind of 'gets it.' She was so pissed off when she heard this, so she went home and asked her son, 'Is this true?' And he said, 'Oh yeah, people use that word all the time!'" The casualness with which their children's peers employed such racial epithets was surprising to both Eunice and her white friend, especially given the ostensibly progressive environment. Visaka, a South Asian woman, reported that her daughter had also encountered some explicitly racist prejudice at school: "I think [she] feels a lot of it because she actually identifies as American. She doesn't identify as [South Asian]. She came home crying because one of her school friends told her she was going to have to go back to her country, that Trump is going to build a wall, and she is not going to be able to live here any longer. So, I had a talk with her and with the teachers. I said: 'She's American.'" The exclusionary treatment her daughter received left Visaka disillusioned about her assumption that generational change would ameliorate her exposure to this type of encounter: "It was sad for me because, as an adult, I feel different all the time. I was hoping it would be a different experience for my child. But what can you do? People are people." Although Visaka did not appear to internalize the racist messages of such treatment, her response seemed to reflect a fatalism about the possibility that she and her family would ever be fully accepted as members of their new community.

While much of the explicit racism experienced by many of my interviewees was interpersonal, many noted various Upper Valley institutions that also engaged in systematically devaluing and discriminatory practices. According to Sarah, a Filipina nurse who had been living in the Upper Valley for three years, her professional advancement at the hospital where she worked had repeatedly been blocked because of her ethnicity: "I said to my nurse manager, 'How can I get to that [higher-level] post?' She said to me in plain, simple language, 'You can never get there because you're Filipino.' It doesn't matter if I improve my qualifications, or if I do a better job, or [demonstrate] leadership. Those things don't matter at all." In addition to her frustration at not being able to advance in her job, Sarah was shocked and hurt to learn that, even within her professional community of nurses, her credentials and skills were not considered the most important criteria for advancement. Emma, a Black woman who had lived in the Upper Valley for more than a decade, described encountering similar professional roadblocks in the region, particularly in advancing beyond an initial job interview when applying for jobs for which she was clearly well qualified:

> When I was living in New York, I was never unemployed for more than what felt like five minutes. It was easy for me to get work based on my

skill set. When I came up here as a freelancer, I would reach out to people, and they would see my work and I would get great feedback. Then, the moment I would meet them, the meeting was over before it began. I have had numerous interviews like that. It got to the point where I put my photo on my resume. I was like, you know what, I'm so tired of getting good feedback and phone interviews, and then I meet them, and they take one look at me and no matter what I say, it's done. It feels like too much of a psychic burden to go through that. So, I was like, let me just weed out who I know isn't going to be interested in me.

It was hard for Emma not to see these experiences as clearly tied to her racial identity as a Black woman, given the difference in the response to her qualifications in this predominantly white area and in the more racially diverse New York City. Although Emma did finally land a job, doing so had necessitated applying for a position that she knew she was "overqualified for. But I was like, I need a job! It's a support position, and I'm still in that. It's still hourly. It's like, is it just me? Are other people going through this? I hate making assumptions, but it just it seems odd to me." Despite seeming to want to wish away the implied racism behind these repeated rejections and having to settle for a lower-paying and lower-prestige job, she was ultimately compelled to interpret it as a statement about her perceived value to the community.

Another form of explicit institutional racism observed by people of color I interviewed was the refusal of many of the local secondary schools to change their Native-themed mascots despite growing recognition of the psychological harm that such stereotypes perpetuate on those with Indigenous and other minoritized identities. This lack of cultural sensitivity and the burden of education it places on those affected were demonstrated by a story that Margaret, a middle-aged Native American woman who had lived in the Upper Valley since she was a teenager, told about her mother's efforts to change her high school's mascot:

When we first moved here, they had the Raiders, which had an Indian head on it. When my brother entered high school, my mother fought the school to get it taken off. The school didn't like the change because it had been there forever, generation after generation. They kept the name, but they changed the mascot to a Viking. People would stand up and ask my mom why she felt this way, and she explained that it was racist. But people just had a hard time understanding that, especially because it had been acceptable for so long.

Despite Margaret's mother's success in getting the school to change the mascot, a testament to her strength and willingness to pursue change and educate her neighbors, fifteen years later a number of high schools in and near the Upper Valley still retain racist names and mascots.[3] The failure of longtime residents, whether out of nostalgia or ignorance, to consider the consequences of retaining a mascot or name that perpetuates stereotypical and dehumanizing imagery serves to preserve their own comfort while prohibiting residents of color from feeling the same comfort.

Several interviewees also recounted frequent and unjustified experiences with racialized surveillance. Saima, a Middle Eastern Muslim woman who had lived in her town for a couple of years, told of being unsettled by repeated racial profiling, such as a series of incidents in which it seemed very clear to her and her husband that they were being profiled because of their Muslim and Arab American identities:

> You know what they do with me and my husband? They have a [US Census] guy, and he keeps coming to us every few months and checks on us, like, "Where do you work?" After several months I said, "Do you do this to everyone in this building?" And he said, "No. You were randomly selected." I swear, when we come home, he is downstairs waiting for us. The last time, my husband got angry and said, "Enough. We don't want to do it anymore." Then they called us by phone and said, "Here will be someone who is better to talk with you." It was another white guy, and he basically said, "Hey, I have visited your country." I think he said India or something like that. And I was just like, "Oh my god, he literally lumped us all up together in one." And so, my husband hung up. When they called me, I did answer, "Yes, we are still working and yes, we still live in the same place." And he goes, "That's it. We won't call you anymore." And then two weeks ago, they call us again and they say, "I'm so sorry. I don't know how you were randomly selected this year again." And I said, "Nope. There is no way we were randomly selected. Please don't call me anymore." I do think, why are they choosing us? Something's going on with us.

Saima and her husband suspected their ethnic and religious identities were not only devalued but considered potentially threatening, making them feel singled out and distrusted in the community.

In another example, Emma reported having been surveilled by local police with such frequency that she worried about walking in a group with other people of color:

> When I first landed here, police would follow me around. At first it was like, oh wow, they are really kind of present. Then I was like, they are driving very slowly behind me. When I was walking with my friend, we were followed by the county sheriff back and forth. We finally called the [local] police to confirm that we were okay to be walking. We are two middle-aged women trying to burn some calories! That's all we were doing. That doesn't happen when I'm with a white person. This is why I want to start Girl Trek, where primarily Black females get together to walk for their health. It's usually like ten females or more. I'll see how that goes over in the Upper Valley!

Although Emma's proposed women's walking group seemed to brush off the surveillance in a lighthearted way, she later admitted that she found such encounters with the police traumatizing: "I feel very concerned. I really make an effort to calm myself. We pick up on nervousness, just like an animal would. So, if I get pulled over, I really do my best to just center myself so that it minimizes their fear. Like, *they* shouldn't feel afraid of *me*. People do stupid things when they are afraid. But yeah, getting followed, that's just like . . . they're the ones with the gun, not me, so it makes me feel very unsafe."

According to Steven, a Black man who had lived in the Upper Valley for seven years, these kinds of frequent and unwarranted surveillance further reinforced his feeling that the Upper Valley is not really home: "It's hard to feel like home when I'm stopped multiple times by the police. It would be one thing if I got stopped and got tickets. But when I get stopped, it's constantly, 'Okay, everything checks out.' I don't know if I feel like home when you constantly harass me. There's no outcome of I need to change my behavior [or] there's something wrong with my car. You are just stopping me for the sake of stopping me." Steven found it particularly galling that none of those multiple police stops resulted in tickets, which to him indicated that he had been surveilled simply because, as a Black man, he had been deemed by the police as a potential threat to the peace and comfort of a predominantly white community.

In general, the interviewees appeared surprised and unsettled by the explicit racism they had encountered even in the left-leaning core Upper Valley towns in which most of them lived and worked. While such explicitness runs counter to more widespread subtle and covert means of socially keeping racial and ethnic minorities "in their place," the more obvious intent of such encounters seemed to make it easier for interviewees to identify and respond to than the more ambiguous mechanisms of misrecognition they also reported.

Social Distance

A less overt form of social boundary-setting on the part of longtime white residents that resulted in misrecognition of the full humanity and contributions of newcomers of color in the Upper Valley is social distance, or a sense of remoteness or unfamiliarity between social groups. Although the indicators of social distance reported by the interviewees were often subtle and only rarely overtly unkind or racist, they nonetheless operated to assign people of color to a marginal social position by making them feel invisible or unimportant. As their reported experiences revealed, social distance operates on three main dimensions observed by social scientists—interactive, affective, and normative—that often overlap and reinforce one another to increase interviewees' sense of exclusion from the larger community.

The aspect of social distance that the interviewees mentioned most often was interactive, referring to the frequency or degree of interaction among individuals from different groups. Greg, a middle-aged biracial man who had come to identify with his Native ancestry largely because he was so often perceived as non-white by other people,[4] reported that he had managed to make some friends since moving across the country to settle in the area with his family seven years ago but that most of those friends were what he called other "transplants," people who, like him, had moved to the area to work for Dartmouth College or Dartmouth Health: "Most of the friends that I have met here are . . . there's a doctor, a pharmacist, an engineer . . . only one [of them] is from here."

While acknowledging that he and his "transplant" professional friends, most of whom were also people of color, were extended a certain level of acceptance by most residents of the area, Greg still seemed to find that acceptance tenuous: "I don't know if you are welcome because you are welcome, or if you get a pass because people respect your degree." Greg thus described himself as an "accepted guest" in the community and observed that longtime residents did not appear to be very interested in taking their relationship with him to the next level and becoming friends: "They already have their people. If they don't already know you, they won't look at you twice." His chosen strategy for forming connections was making friends with other parents at his children's school, as "that seemed to be the only way to circumvent the culture." Greg attributed the social distance that longtime residents kept from him to the area's more general culture of reserve and assimilative pressure to adhere to normative status characteristics, which he contrasted to his experience growing up in the West, where the culture was "more relaxed, less closed-off. You can meet someone through whatever avenue, and there's no boxes that you have to fit into or whatever." Although he had managed to make some friends in the Upper Valley, Greg was not willing to go so far as to call it home: "Not really. I guess it feels kind of more like grad school did. Like, all right, you're going to be here for a while, so make yourself at home. If I'm thinking more from an attachment perspective, I don't feel like this is home." As a result, Greg predicted he would probably stay in the Upper Valley at least until his kids finished high school but felt so unattached that, if he had to leave before then for some reason, "it wouldn't be a big deal."

Other interviewees also reported that longtime residents often appeared to avoid contact and association with them. Eunice, who had lived in her town for sixteen years, shared Greg's observation that the Upper Valley's culture of reserve tended to make it particularly hard for newcomers to break into existing social circles:

My experience of the Upper Valley is that there is a lot of cliquey-ness. I mean there are a lot of long-standing friend groups; social interaction tends to be very group-y. I don't mean cliquey like mean girls or anything, although there is some of that, but cliquey in that there are a lot of things that people do as groups. Human beings are social, people have groupings everywhere. But there is a closeness and solidity and boundary to the

groupings here. People are a little surprised at how standoffish people are
and how hard it is to make friends.

Although Eunice had eventually managed to make friends in the community,
she too reported that most of those friendships were with other newcomers to
town, whom she noted were also more likely to eventually leave the area than
long-time residents.

Anura, an Indian woman who had lived in her town for twelve years, recalled how difficult she and her family had found it to form connections with
others in the community, especially in the beginning: "My in-laws visited,
and they were like, 'How can you live here?' We had hardly any social life.
I hardly met anybody." When one of their children was diagnosed with significant learning difficulties, they had begun "thinking maybe we would be
better off going back home because at least we would be with family," but they
decided to stay because of the school-related resources and services available
there for their child, despite the lack of emotional and instrumental support
they received from others in the community. Eventually, with an exertion of
effort—particularly her husband's volunteering to teach in the elementary
school's supplementary science program—Anura felt they had become more
accepted as members of the community, demonstrating the way that a visible
commitment to shared values, such as a belief in education, can reduce social
distance (Hoekstra and Gerteis 2019).

But other people of color reported that time and effort had not always led
to more or closer social relationships. Yuyan, who had immigrated from China
and reported still feeling very alone after thirteen years in her town, described
wanting less social distance from longtime residents than they seemed to want
to keep from her:

> I feel that people keep a good distance. They have more personal space
> than I need. I feel isolated in an island of myself. I still feel like I am alone
> a lot of time. I don't feel comfortable to sort of break the boundaries they
> grew up with. It is just like "Hi" and a smile. I don't know if they just
> generally like to have that kind of distance to feel safe. They seem to carry
> around the boundary like a shell, like a wall. It is hard to penetrate.

Yuyan's description of the lack of reciprocity she had experienced with her
neighbors made it sound almost as if longtime residents lived within a gated

community, meeting their emotional and practical needs among themselves and protected from those outside by a wall without a key or code for entry and thereby leaving Yuyan and others like her feeling forever locked out. Ayana, for her part, seemed surer that the similar interactional distance that white residents maintained from her was related primarily to her non-white identity:

> When I walk out, nobody really makes an effort to speak to me. I can tell you honestly, I don't think I have ever just been greeted by somebody who is not Black. I am from the Midwest and South, and we have this hospitality ingrained in us. So, it's natural for me to meet you with a smile and say, "Hello, how are you doing?" But when somebody doesn't speak to you or doesn't acknowledge you, and then a white woman could walk in, but the greeting is very different . . .

Ayana's experience thus suggests that the interactive social distance and perceived lack of connection that a number of the respondents of color linked to Northern New England's culture of reserve may be particularly marked for people of color.

A second dimension of social distance observed by the interviewees, affective or emotional distance, was related more specifically to the tenor of interactions among people and particularly to a lack of sympathy for and acceptance of members of groups other than one's own. Jocelyn, a US-born Filipina American, reported frequently facing this form of social distance in her social encounters within the Upper Valley and attributed it primarily to others not seeing her as a complex person because of her racial identity: "Being able to move through a space and not have to be so hypervigilant all the time is a privilege afforded when you are a part of a majority. Here, I feel very visible. People notice me, but I don't know if they understand me in the way that I want to be understood." Feeling similarly visible and invisible at the same time, Emma also reported that white community members seemed invested in keeping an affective distance from her and other people of color:

> There are some folks that I can tell by just body language alone, and sometimes even by their actions, that I am not part of their "New England Dream." For some people [that dream is] to try to escape diversity, really, by coming up to areas that are predominantly white. So, primarily my connections have been with other transplants, other people who have

relocated here. I know how it feels to be on the outside, and so when I see
another individual or groups of people being othered in some way, I do try
to go out of my way as much as possible to create an environment that's
like, "I see you. You are not invisible to me." I have a neighbor who is a
person of color, and I feel like I never have to explain myself.

As Emma related later in our conversation, even her husband, who is white,
did not always seem to fully "get it," which often led her to call upon her relationships with other people of color to fulfill her need to be fully seen during
social interactions.

The third dimension of social distance observed by the people of color interviewed for this study is normative, which refers to applying a set of collec-
tively recognized judgments to determine what types of people and behaviors
are considered acceptable for group membership and thus to draw distinctions
between *us* and *them*, *insider* and *outsider*. The operations of this particular
process were evident in numerous interviewees' stories about attempts to connect with long-standing community members that appeared to fail because of
the newcomers' seeming inability to fulfill various expectations of the local
culture. For instance, Joseph, a Chinese American physician, reported that
he had tried to make friends by joining "a big hockey group that plays every
Sunday. I tried out, but it was a lot more intense than I thought. They were
like, 'Oh, it's very laid back.' But it wasn't. I was not up to par." Even though he
had been invited to play hockey with this long-standing group, he believed that
the acceptance it suggested had actually hinged on a demonstration of facility
with a culturally white, northern sport that he was unable to provide. Describing a similar dynamic, Hayden reported that locals would sometimes ask him
to participate in their cultural events or activities but did not reciprocate with
an interest in his: "Because [New England has] a very rich, very deep culture,
there has been a lot of adapting on my part. When you meet people here, [they
are] like, 'Oh, let me teach you how to make maple syrup. Let me teach you
old hymns.' But in terms of the flip side and people getting to know where I'm
from and the sorts of things that make me *me*, I wouldn't say that people are
too keen on it." Observing such residents' apparent sense of entitlement to set
the cultural standards for what is admired and shared as "traditional" in the

community, Hayden felt unseen as he sensed his own cultural celebrations to be outside the norm.

While most of these interviewees had moved to the Upper Valley hoping to settle and develop fulfilling relationships in their new home, many felt pushed to the social margins because of their perceived differences from longtime white residents. Although cultivating relationships with other "transplants" served as a survival mechanism and kept them from personalizing the poor treatment they received, that choice also seemed to foreclose their prospects for gaining respect, appreciation, and full membership in the broader community.

Provisional Acceptance

A third main mechanism of misrecognition, provisional acceptance, consists of repeated situations in which people of color are required to prove themselves worthy of respect in their social interactions with members of the white community. As the term connotes, such acceptance is granted only cautiously, taking a "we shall see" approach that insinuates that social membership must be earned and remains conditional. A number of the interviewees of color recounted stories of social interactions with white residents of the Upper Valley that seemed to require them to earn or justify their position as respected, worthy, and valuable individuals within the community, in the process reminding them of and maintaining their subordinate status. Ethnographer Elijah Anderson has likened such interpersonal performances to a dance in which people of color are initially seen by white people as suspicious and must overcome a "deficit of credibility" before being even conditionally accepted (2015, 13).

Perhaps none of the interviewees' stories demonstrated the operations and effects of this mechanism more than those of Saima, who had moved to the Upper Valley when her partner was recruited for a high-profile professional position and at the time of our interview had lived in her town for two years. Racially, Saima identified as "a Brown Arab woman, African, definitely not white," a nonnormative identity based primarily on other residents' perceiving and reacting to her as neither white nor American. As evidence of this perception, she reported that her conversations with new people in the area typically began with their asking her, "Where are you from?" In response, she would often give the name of the African country from which her family had immigrated "because I know that's what they mean. But growing up, my mother would always say, 'Don't tell anyone where you're from! Always just say American.' But the faces people made when I said that! I was just like, I can't say this anymore. I'm just so used to it, but obviously it has the implication that I don't belong here."

Saima experienced such negotiations around her identity as a proving ground in which her membership in the community was considered provisional upon her demonstrating that she was a non-threatening person, and particularly that she was not *that kind* of Muslim American. In the predominantly white, rural setting of the Upper Valley, it was unusual to see a woman wearing a hijab, and Saima was acutely aware that doing so led people to hold a lot of inaccurate assumptions about her:

> They think I *have* to dress the way I do, that I'm submissive, and backwards, really. Because I'm something they're not used to, they think I must come from some strange culture. And they overexaggerate their responses. No matter what it is, they just overexaggerate it. Whether it's me just walking in a supermarket and people stopping to go, "You are sooo beautiful." And I [think to myself], "You mean, I'm just sooo different?" Because that's what it is. It's like I'm a freak, in a way. People may think it's a compliment. If someone calls you beautiful, it's a compliment. But to me, that's not what it's about. It's more like, "I have an image about what you should be, and you're not that. So, I'm praising you."

Saima interpreted this kind of fawning, exoticizing praise as simply a means of allowing white people in the community to feel comfortable with her distinctiveness and to neutralize the implicit threat of her Muslim identity, while in the process making her acceptance by that community provisional upon her acting the part of a "submissive" and "backwards" Muslim woman.

Saima worked as an organizer for a local community group, doing advocacy work around immigration and economic justice issues. Yet even at her job, where Saima was surrounded by left-leaning, activist colleagues, she found that her coworkers tended to accept her only as long as she did not conform to stereotypes typically associated with Muslim people: "When I started working, they were like, 'When we first saw you, we saw a Muslim woman. And by the end of the interview, we saw an organizer!' To me, that means they still have a problem with Muslims. Saying 'who happens to be Muslim' is the same thing as saying, 'You happen to have this quality that's not good.' Things like that are an indication that you have a problem with racism." In her role as an organizer, she also found that her coworkers and other activists with whom she interacted would often ask her to "share her story," which she saw as a way of asking her to prove she is non-threatening:

> Something else that I noticed: everyone is constantly asking me to share my story. Like, where I came from, what I've been through. I'm at a place right now where I am kind of tired of sharing my story. It's a show for them! It's like going to the movie theater, where you're going to enjoy something. And the more I share about the trauma, the more it's like they're getting their [money's] worth or something. I do know that for some reason I score points when I share.

In Saima's view, being accepted and valued by the members of the white community with whom she interacted often seemed provisional upon her willingness to repeatedly share her trauma and risk the emotional exhaustion that doing so involved.

In contrast, Saima reported, she found herself less accepted when she acted in ways that dispelled people's assumptions about her mild disposition:

> I am almost positive that I got my job because they thought I was submissive. They thought that, just because I was nice, I was going to go with the flow. I'm blunt, I know that. I am here for those who are being harmed—that's where my heart is. I don't give a shit, to be honest—I don't give a damn about people in power. I can sit with them, but the next day I can call them out. Easy. Now [that they have realized that], it's like my opinion is always questioned. It's always like, "Where did you get your information?" I am too extreme for them.

According to Saima, the unacknowledged racism and resistance to change underlying the provisional nature of her acceptance in the Upper Valley "goes back to the culture here. There are so many well-intentioned people, but when you start to really explain why things are unfair, they're not willing to change it. It's kind of like, 'We want to do good, but when it comes down to it, I'm not doing *that* though. I'm not giving up my privilege. We want to continue being the white people in charge.' They like the power structures the way they are." Saima's experiences illuminate the connection between the cultural environment and the misrecognition she and other newcomers reported encountering, demonstrating how seemingly small interpersonal interactions work together to preserve the superior status position of white people, even among those whose work is to advocate for progressive change and true integration.

After being recruited for jobs whose anticipated rewards had not materialized, both she and her husband were feeling burned out from their constant struggles with coworkers and others in the community. To cope, she reported, they had been trying to spend as much time as possible in non-white spaces where they did not feel required to prove their worth in each interaction:

> Home to me is walking into a place and not having to feel like I'm abnormal, and usually that happens around people of color. With the Black community, the Latinx community, I don't have to prove anything. I don't even have to explain. They're just like, "We get it. We understand. We are under that same kind of crap as well." Even when I cut my hair, I prefer to go to a place that does Black hair. And not because of my hair texture, but because every single time I sit with a white person who cuts my hair it's like, "Tell me about your family. When did you come to the US?" It's almost [as if they are saying], "I want to understand you. You're so odd and so different." And then when I sit with a Black woman who cuts my hair it's like, "Hey, how are you? How was your day?" It's not like I have to prove anything, prove I'm normal or prove my culture is normal. It's just an automatic acceptance. So, feeling at home is just walking into a place and not feeling that I have to prove anything to be treated normally. It's like we're given a criminal card until we prove we're normal.

Like Emma, Saima found herself most at home with other people of color who "get" her and her experiences without explanation or emotional labor.

Among the people of color I interviewed, such experiences of being subjected to provisional acceptance often manifested or began as a generalized feeling of being noticed as different, as standing out from the crowd. Georgia, a Black woman who had lived in the Upper Valley for three years, reported often feeling perceived as odd or abnormal when she was out and about doing her daily activities in the Upper Valley:

> Sometimes when you go into a place and it's off the beaten path [farther from the core of the Upper Valley], you'll get a few more stares, a few more glances. You notice that they are looking at you like, "What is she doing here, or where does she come from?" Sometimes people just stare. I would hate to say that they have never seen an African American before, except for on TV, but sometimes that is how it feels. And the community that I came from was very diverse, and you had a mixture of incomes and races. It was a mixing pot, a perfect mixing pot. Now that I am gone, I realize how perfect it was.

Being repeatedly stared at in public reminded Georgia that other people perceived her as exotic and seemed to confirm that they viewed her as somehow less than human, as undeserving of basic norms of civility.

According to Steven, people of color did not necessarily have to be very far "off the beaten path" within the Upper Valley to be noticed as different:

> Often, I will go into stores and people ask if I am from around here. And I think that's interesting because they didn't ask the two people that walked in ahead of me. I wonder what [it is] about me [that] makes them ask that question, when my license plate, for better or for worse, is New Hampshire. Yet they think of me as the outsider. I think that is in some ways a self-fulfilling prophecy. People don't think I am from here. So, I'm like, well you know, maybe I'm not. There is this unsettling feeling when people ask me. It is asked in a way that is clouded or couched. So, I usually try to react to help them think critically about what they want to ask. I say: "What are you asking specifically? What does 'around here' mean? Is that the planet? What terms are we talking about?" I push the question back to them and force them to think.

For Steven, the repeated assumption that he was not a fellow resident of the Upper Valley was not merely an annoyance but a contributing factor in his growing lack of desire to make the area his permanent home.

According to several other people of color, local residents seemed to not only notice but to be suspicious of them because of their racial difference.

Meisa, a fourth-generation Japanese American who had lived in her town for four years, described what she interpreted as a certain level of distrust on the part of others when she was out in public:

> I feel like they treat me in a certain way, and the only reason I can think of is because I am Asian. For instance, I took my stepdaughter to one of those movies—it was one of those days where school wasn't in, so they had a free movie and gave you little vouchers for free popcorn. I wasn't hungry when we went in, so I didn't get the popcorn. But about twenty minutes into the movie, I got up and I went to the counter. The kid looked at me kind of confused. And the manager came over and he said, "You can only get one." I said, "I haven't gotten anything yet. That's why I have this voucher." I could tell he didn't believe me. I don't know what he thought, I have no idea. But I didn't see him do it to anyone else, so it made me feel as though it was because I was Asian.

Meisa's twinge of doubt as to whether racism was responsible for this response demonstrates how mentally tiring residents of color often find ruminating on these experiences, turning them over in their heads to determine whether the root cause of the poor treatment they have received is truly due to their race and what, if anything, they might have done to avoid it.

Yet other interviewees reported that being viewed as outsiders to the local culture by longtime residents made them feel forced to prove they, too, are insiders who understand the system in order to be deemed worthy of acceptance. Saima, for instance, reported feeling as if she was constantly being asked to demonstrate her commonality with others in the community: "Everyone thinks that I have an accent before I talk. People ask where I am from all the time. And sometimes people will literally say, in line, 'I don't think she speaks English.' I'm like, this is too much." Sarah, a nurse from the Philippines, reported that her perceived foreignness often made her feel out of place in her chosen church community, even after being a member for three years: "It takes a lot before my voice is heard. It goes in here [gesturing to one ear], and it goes out the other. I don't like that. When I first entered the church, I remember being looked at from head to foot and it didn't feel good. As soon as I was able to do all the responses in English and sing the verses in the songs, I made a point for them to hear it." Responding to what she perceived as a challenge to her belonging within her church community, Sarah felt it necessary to publicly perform her status as an insider loudly enough for all to hear. Samuel, who was Haitian-born and had lived in his town for fifteen years, viewed such situations as exams he was required to pass in order to be deemed worthy of respect and belonging:

> Of course, you get tested every now and then. And it is such a familiar place. You can automatically tell the minute the questions start coming. You can tell that they don't think you belong here or don't think you need to be here. I'll give you an example. This gentleman come to my office: "Man, where you from?" "Well, I was born in Haiti." "Oh! But how did you get here?" I said, "Oh man, it's a long story. Been here for a long, long time." And he says, "I see you got a veteran license plate in your car. Are you a veteran?" "Yeah, I was in the military." He said, "Haitian Navy?" I said, "No. United States military, sir. I'm a full veteran." "You mean in our army *here*?" "Yes, sir." I call him sir, give him the grade, because it's not a joke now. You need to be serious with people like that. I'll never forget. I know he was p-h-i-s phishing. And whenever they're phishing like that, of course this is your opportunity to set the record straight. Don't look at people just because of where they come from and think that they may not be part of [this country]. I shed blood for this nation. The freedom that you're enjoying, I am part of that freedom. I gave it to you. So don't come provoke.

Despite being born elsewhere, Samuel had reason to believe that serving the United States in war amply demonstrated his loyalty to and willingness to sacrifice for the people of this nation, and thus being intensely questioned about his right to membership in this country and community served as a particularly potent reminder for him that his racial identity continued to function as a barrier to inclusion.

This sense of being only provisionally accepted led even some longtime residents of color to wonder whether they would ever cease to be considered outsiders by longtime white residents and thus whether the Upper Valley would ever fully feel like home. When I asked Zayyan, an Indonesian woman who had lived in her town for fifteen years, whether she felt valued in her community, she equivocated: "Uhhh, yes? And no. Well, when I meet people on a surface level in this community, I don't know that I feel valued because they immedi-

ately question where I'm from. They don't assume that I'm from here." It was
specifically the assumption that she is not part of the Upper Valley, despite
her decade and a half residence in her town, that caused Zayyan to feel devalued. Similarly, Robbie, a US-born Mexican American who had moved to his
town while in high school and had lived in the Upper Valley for two decades,
expressed how tiresome he found it when people assumed he was an outsider.
"I'm like, 'I'm from Washington state.' Then, they're always like, 'Oh. Well,
your parents . . .' I always try to give them a hard time before I answer. I get
upset about it, but it's not worth my time, so I just answer." Robbie's attempts
to push back against such questions, if briefly and kindly, were intended both
to educate those who inquired about his status as a member of the community
and to call attention to the presumptuousness of their request that he prove his
insider status. Even though Zayyan and Robbie clearly thought of the Upper
Valley as their home, being repeatedly subject to such questioning was a continual reminder that at least some other people did not see them the same way.

A number of Black women reported that others' faulty assumptions about
their financial resources seemed to be the basis of yet another form of having
to prove themselves to gain acceptance. Ayana, for instance, shared a detailed
story about being mistaken as an unserious buyer while trying to purchase a
car in the Upper Valley:

> Typically, car salesmen are pushy. As soon as they see somebody come on
> the lot, they come up and say, "Is there anything I can help you with?" So,
> I'm looking at the cars and I'm walking around, circling the lot. I'm like,
> okay, maybe they're just busy inside. So, I walk inside, and I see three dif-
> ferent people just scrolling on their phones. I ask the front desk and they're
> like, "Okay, we will have somebody out to meet you." Fifteen minutes go
> by, and I'm like, okay, do you all not want a sale? I was really confused.
> So, finally, this woman just sees me standing outside, probably awkwardly,
> because I don't even know what to do with myself. She comes out and she
> was like, "Is there anything I can help you with?" And I was like, "Yeah, I
> was trying to find somebody to help me." She was like, "Oh, I didn't even
> know. I can help you." Then throughout the entire sales process, I noticed
> how they were a lot more hands-on—wanted to know more and how they
> could help—with the white counterparts that were walking in versus me.
> I don't know if [they thought], "Oh, her credit is probably shot, let's not
> even bother." My credit score is great, by the way. But they didn't know me

from a can of paint. All they saw was my Black skin, and maybe they made some kind of stereotypical judgment that I wasn't a serious buyer. I just thought, never mind, and took my business elsewhere. I bought a car the very next weekend at a dealership in Connecticut. They were absolutely amazing. Granted, I had to drive six hours, but I would do that rather than ever go to another dealership that is within five minutes of my home in the Upper Valley. That was an experience that really opened my eyes up to this area. Not only do you not care for me as a person, but you don't care for me enough to even let me invest in a business? That, to me, spoke volumes.

Following a common arc in such provisional acceptance incidents, Ayana's story moves from being perplexed by the way she was being treated in a public setting to becoming annoyed and angry at being dismissed as unworthy and finally to having to decide what action to take to maintain her dignity in the situation—which in this case was taking her business elsewhere, even though it came at a substantial personal cost. Her story offers a clear example of how being misrecognized as less worthy exerts a significant toll on people of color that is not exacted upon white individuals in the Upper Valley.

Other Black women reported similar instances in which salespeople failed to see them as valuable or trustworthy customers. In one such example, Camila, a Black woman of Caribbean ancestry who had lived in her town for three years, described repeated instances of poor service at the makeup counter of an Upper Valley department store:

They were not helping me right away and I would have to ask for help. And then, when I asked for a sample, sometimes they would act like they didn't want to give me samples. Then one of my friends came in, she's an Afro-Latina, and they were giving her the same attitude they would give me. A third time I went in with one of my colleagues who is Indian, they were doing the same thing. So, this was three different times that this happened, and I observed them not doing this to other people. I wanted to go back into the store the last time it happened, and my colleague said, "No, no, no. Let's not go in." But I was still upset. So, when we got to her house, I called back to the store, and I said, "This is what has been going on. It is unacceptable. I have been a VIP member for years and years and years. I have spent probably thousands of dollars over the last twenty to thirty years." And the manager said, "I am so sorry. No one should feel that way. I am going to speak to my staff. I apologize." I have to be careful of how

I represent myself when I'm speaking up, because I don't want to offend anybody. But I had to say, "We are professional people. I don't understand why we are being treated this way." It really took me aback, but I didn't let it stop me. It's like you want to be on guard. You just don't know if somebody is going to accept you because you don't look like them. It was uncomfortable, but I was like, this is the closest town that has things that I need, so I am just going to have to push through.

Camila not only ties this repeated poor treatment to her non-white racial identity, but her response illuminates the emotional toll of having to constantly be "on guard" to detect and deflect others' lack of acceptance. Although Camila found having to assert her status as a professional person uncomfortable, she deemed it worth doing to gain the respect she and her colleagues of color have a right to expect as they go about meeting their life necessities in the Upper Valley.

Emma reported repeatedly being followed in stores and having her currency checked to ensure it was not counterfeit:

As soon as I went into the store, a couple minutes later I was being followed. It was very obvious. That's a clear message that I'm not welcome in that space. I'm trying not to even carry cash around anymore because this is so disturbing. I get my bills counterfeit-checked almost all the time. I have even had a ten-dollar bill get counterfeit-checked. And I have seen my white partner use a twenty or a fifty and not get checked. First of all, it's really insulting because I am a very honest person. But is this done for everyone? If this is done for everyone, then fine. But the person in front of you didn't get their bill checked and the person behind you ain't getting their bill checked.

Because she witnessed white people receiving very dissimilar treatment, Emma had no doubt that this misrecognition—her not being viewed as the honest person she knew herself to be—stemmed from her identity as a Black woman.

Not even their professional occupational status protected interviewees from this form of misrecognition, and several reported interactions with clients and other residents who questioned their credentials and right to occupy their positions. Visaka, a South Asian woman who had lived in the state for seventeen years, described regularly feeling disrespected in her professional capacity: "I feel like I have to prove myself. They naturally think that I am somebody's assistant. Once, I was meeting a client for the first time and two minutes after meeting him he says, 'Are you a citizen?' I was happy to share my status. But in a professional environment like that you don't expect people to just blurt out, 'Are you a citizen? Are you legal?' I thought it was really crass for someone to look at me and just say that." Despite laughing at the ridiculousness of the client's actions as she told the story, Visaka appeared deeply affected by the client's disrespect. Chimaobi, a Nigerian immigrant, also reported having his credentials as a college professor challenged by people in the community: "One person commented, 'Why would you be teaching American students since English is their first language? Why not foreign students?' I explained how writing is a different kind of discourse. Even if you speak the language of instruction, you still have to understand the codes of writing. When I talk about some of the things I do here, there is a way that [others] will sort of push it aside. It is kind of implicit." Chimaobi's having earned a doctoral degree in English apparently was not a sufficient credential to satisfy those who questioned his expertise and deservingness to hold his position.

Questioning the professional contributions of people of color seemed to be especially prevalent within academic spaces, settings in which equal educational attainment might be expected to diminish, if not erase, status differences based on race. Emma, for instance, described several situations in which her questions or expertise were deemed less important or valid than those of her white colleagues: "Recently I was at a talk. In the Q&A, my hand went up right away because there was someone on the panel that said something really meaningful that I wanted to ask about. There were like four or five rounds of people raising their hands, and this woman would not pick me. She just would not choose me. In those spaces, our voices don't count."

Steven offered a similar example of an academic workplace interaction in which he felt misperceived and devalued by his colleagues:

I try to reflect what's happening in the room. So, if someone's talking softly, I might I adjust how I am communicating to reflect the timbre or the pace of the conversation that is happening in the room. So, I remember vividly, I was in a healthy discourse around some topic area. I'm like, "Oh yeah, this is exciting!" I actually like when people pick apart my ideas. I think that's where innovation and real creative problem-solving happens. So, I am really invested in this conversation. And the person raises their voice, so I raise my voice. I'm actually excited. Good mood, good day. And so, the meeting concludes and I'm [thinking], "I had a decent time of articulating myself, positioning my thoughts and positing my ideas." And so, I am walking back to my office and three people follow me to my office and say to me, "You know, you seemed really upset in the meeting." And I said, "Oh, interesting. Help me understand what presented to you as upset." And they said, you know, this, this, this, and this. I just couldn't believe that their conclusions were that I was upset. I am like, nothing could be further from the truth. I will forever remember that because I didn't jump to conclusions. I asked them, "Are you going to talk to that colleague who was in that dialogue?" And they were like, "No, they seemed fine." I'm even pretty sure I was smiling. I was actually happy to be in that conversation. I don't know what trope or stereotype they were applying, but it has to be something.

This exchange suggested to Steven not only that his peers did not understand him in the same way he understood himself but that they interpreted his behavior through a different lens than that applied to his white colleague. Their interpretation of the interaction appeared to be colored by Steven's racial identity as a Black man, leading them to perceive his engagement as angry or threatening and requiring their intervention to diffuse what they thought was a tense situation. Steven's acceptance into the group thus appeared to be provisional upon a willingness to change his behavior to be meeker than that of his white colleagues and as certainly less energetic than was his natural inclination, echoing the experiences reported by Saima.

Although some of these examples of the various ways in which newcomers of color found themselves the subject of provisional acceptance involved more obviously rude behavior, others suggest that provisional acceptance might actually be the most pernicious mechanism of misrecognition by allowing white interlocutors to keep people of color in their supposedly subordinate places with outward expressions of niceness and inclusivity. In all its forms, however, it represents and signals an ungenerous reading of another person's potential for membership in an exclusive club and places the burden on them to repeatedly prove their worth or to accept the social costs of not doing so.

———

As this chapter has shown, explicit racism, social distance, and provisional acceptance together operate to misrecognize newcomers of color in the Upper Valley despite their overall high educational attainment and occupational prestige. As such, misrecognition provides the longtime white residents of the area an effective symbolic means through which to marginalize and prevent people of color from accessing the full benefits of and sense of belonging in this rural community. The next chapter examines the emotional consequences of being misrecognized and the ways in which the inability to feel fully at home in the Upper Valley leaves new residents of color feeling homesick.

FOUR

Homesickness

An Emotional Manifestation of Racial Inequality

In a *Black Girl in Maine* blog post, self-proclaimed "disrupter and raconteur" Shay Stewart-Bouley confessed to not feeling at home in Northern New England even after having lived there for more than twenty years. "While . . . I have gained much personally and have grown living here," she confided, "I must confess that it doesn't feel like my *home*. It never has felt like it. . . . How does a middle-aged Black woman make a home and build community in a place where her existence is still an oddity? . . . Always fighting and talking about our quest for humanity. Honestly, it is tiring" (Stewart-Bouley 2022). Like Stewart-Bouley, the people of color interviewed for this book, despite having moved to the Upper Valley with the expectation of making that culturally white place their home, instead found their "quest for humanity"—their yearning to be fully accepted, valued, and integrated into their new community—being repeatedly stymied by misrecognition on the part of longtime residents. Many described the ongoing struggle to belong as emotionally difficult, as captured in Steven's description of the Upper Valley as "a very difficult place to live, grow, and do more than just survive" for people of color such as himself.

This chapter examines the emotional ripple effects of misrecognition among people of color by elucidating the main symptoms of what this book refers to as *homesickness*: the negative feelings and emotions evoked by the inability to think of the place in which one lives as truly home, as a place in which one can feel safe, accepted, and at ease.[1] As the following analysis of interviewees' responses to questions about their mental health and sense of connection to the Upper Valley demonstrates, such feelings of homesickness are a result of receiving repeated reminders, both overt and covert, that other residents do not view them as fully worthy of respect and inclusion in the larger community.[2] Reflecting a social-psychological understanding that individual identities are continually made and remade through such social interactions, these findings regarding the impact of misrecognition vividly illustrate political theorist Charles Taylor's assertion that people can suffer "real damage, real distortion, if the people or society around them mirror back to them a confining or demeaning or contemptible picture of themselves" (1994, 25).[3] In so doing, these impacts also provide additional insight into the seemingly benign practices through which whiteness exerts "symbolic, emotional, and existential" violence on people of color (McDermott and Ferguson 2022, 269). As a result of such symbolic and cultural practices, people of color have been largely excluded from the confident and uncontested claims to home available to white residents of the Upper Valley.

This chapter's investigation of the specific ways in which racial inequality reveals itself in the day-to-day lives of people of color attempting to make a home in the Upper Valley and the ways in which they make meaning out of those experiences begins with an explication of the major emotional symptoms of the homesickness they have experienced, followed by an analysis of various coping mechanisms they reported having developed to avoid or dampen the damaging effects of misrecognition on their mental health and sense of belonging.

Symptoms of Homesickness

As part of this study, each survey and interview participant was asked to self-rate their mental health as excellent, very good, good, fair, or poor, providing a self-rated measure of mental health. Although the majority of those participants rated their mental health as good or better, an examination of differences in the distribution of responses among the interviewees of color and the white survey respondents, as shown in table 4.1, reveals a pattern of racial inequality.[4] Although 30.6 percent of the white residents surveyed for this study rated their mental health as excellent, only 13.8 percent of the interviewees of color did the same. While the share of white individuals in the Upper Valley who rated their mental health as excellent was nearly identical to 31 percent of all Americans who reported the same in a 2022 Gallup poll (Brenan 2022), that of the participants of color was less than half that level. At the other end of the mental health continuum, only 2.8 percent of the white individuals responding to this study's survey rated their mental health as either fair or poor, in contrast to 13.8 percent of the interview respondents of color, or almost five times as many, who answered the same. Together, these differences reflect a broad phenomenon of racialized mental health inequality among residents of the Upper Valley.

Whereas the participants' responses to the self-rated mental health question provided a general measure of their feelings of well-being, happiness, and personal satisfaction, a closer examination of the responses of participants of color to a follow-up question about why they had selected that particular answer and to other interview questions revealed a constellation of experiences and emotional states that appeared to characterize the more general sense of homesickness that many reported. As an analysis of those responses revealed,

TABLE 4.1. **Self-rated mental health among white survey respondents (n=147) and interviewees of color (n=58).**

Rating	White respondents		Non-white respondents	
	N	Percent	N	Percent
Excellent	45	30.6%	8	13.8%
Very good	63	42.9%	23	39.7%
Good	35	23.8%	19	32.8%
Fair	2	1.4%	8	13.8%
Poor	2	1.4%	0	0.0%
Total	147	100.0%	58	100.0%

Source: author's survey and interview data.

the participants' repeated exposure to misrecognition by their fellow residents in the Upper Valley resulted in three main emotional symptoms that demonstrate such homesickness: insecurity, anxiety, and exhaustion.

Insecurity

In discussing their mental health, a number of interviewees reported experiencing a pervasive sense of insecurity, or a lack of what Giddens (1991) has termed "ontological security," a basic sense of comfort, confidence, and trust in the world that is typically achieved when there is continuity between individuals' self-identity and the information they receive from their routine interactions with others (Dupuis and Thorns 1998). In one example of the lack of such security, Teresa, a Latina woman who had lived in the Upper Valley for nine years, recalled a minor health crisis that she described as a wake-up call regarding the precarity of her life in a community in which residents maintain a social distance from one another. "What worries me the most here," she reported, was that "I spend a lot of time alone. Once, I fainted while I was at home, and it was a very shocking experience. When I woke up, the sofa was kind of moved and one of the rocking chairs was flipped over. I hit myself on the coffee table very hard. [I thought to myself], 'Wow, I'm so vulnerable.' Life around here . . . it is a very intense community, and everyone is very busy. So, I just felt like, wow, I'm alone. It's very personal, in a way." Teresa expressly linked her sense of insecurity to one particular mechanism of misrecognition, social distance, which in her case she generously attributed primarily to people in the community being too busy to have time for her.

Several other interviewees described their feelings of insecurity as a lack of confidence in their ability to forge meaningful and supportive relationships with other members of the community. Xiu, a Chinese woman in her early thirties who had moved to the Upper Valley for her first professional job after graduate school, struggled with the fact that even after two years of living in her town, she still had not been able to develop a group of people she could comfortably depend on to just hang out with:

I couldn't find anybody to watch the game with me, so I stayed at home. I know I could have just showed up at a bar and made friends there, but I was just so uncomfortable to go by myself. So, I just sat home and refreshed my Google page and kept the score. It is embarrassing! All my friends in Georgia went to a bar in a group, and they cried, and they laughed. They told me afterwards and I was like, I want to go back so badly and have this sort of camaraderie.

Xiu expressed sadness and embarrassment about being alone for a situation in which she wanted to be sharing emotions and bonding in joy and disappointment. She followed this anecdote with further reflection on the satisfaction she feels from true friendship: "When I talk to my close friends, I am happy because I get to say the things I want to say. I know they are patient to listen to me, and I am more comfortable to say things. But when I am in a larger group [here], I just pull back and don't engage." Xiu's memories of the kind of friendships she had established living elsewhere made her long for connection with people who would give her time to express herself in English and display a genuine interest in her. This reflection reminded her how often she felt forced to stifle her true self in her Upper Valley interactions, as she seemed to worry that she would not be fully accepted if she required too much compassionate energy from people. For Xiu, the thoughts and feelings resulting from social distance created an overall sense of insecurity about her ability to be accepted and comfortable in the community. Akash, a Guyanese American professional in his early twenties, expressed a similar insecurity about the nature of the relationships he had formed in his new community. Though Akash had managed to make some acquaintances in the year he had been living in his town, "One of the things I don't know about is whether I will be able to make as deep friendships and relationships as I had with people who I call my best friends. That is something I'm not sure if I will have with members of this community."

Even though Xiu and Akash were relatively recent arrivals in the Upper Valley, the insecurity they described about their relationships within the community was also echoed by other interviewees who had lived there longer. Those individuals, perhaps because the social distance they experienced had not changed over time, worried about being overlooked or forgotten in this place. Ehsan, a middle-aged Pakistani medical professional who had lived in his town for sixteen years, described how his lack of deep ties with other members of the community had left him feeling adrift:

> I think I worry most about connection. My biggest fear is getting lost
> in this community. Like, I might stay up here a long time, and for some
> reason get kind of disconnected from a job or something and just have no
> one to turn to for any sort of help. I would just kind of get lost in the mix
> of the Upper Valley. Having those deep connections, where people would
> check in and know where I am and be concerned, that is what I worry
> about.

Not even nearly two decades of living in the Upper Valley had been enough for
Ehsan to make the kinds of connections that would lead to others noticing or
being concerned if he disappeared, leaving him feeling detached and unsure
of his place in the community. In a similar vein, Steven, a Black professional
who had lived in town for seven years, expressed how his lack of close relationships made him feel vulnerable: "Am I going to die alone? Am I going to be
harassed? I think either of those." He went on to relate these worries to the
local culture: "This is something that is very distinct about New England that
I don't love. There is a Baldwin quote where the thrust of the argument is 'It
is the silence of your friends that you remember, the indifference of people.'"
Although Steven's intended point appeared to combine sentiments from two
different quotations—Martin Luther King, Jr.'s "In the end, we will remember
not the words of our enemies, but the silence of our friends" and James Baldwin's "And part of the rage is this: It isn't only what is happening to you. But
it's what's happening all around you and all of the time in the face of the most
extraordinary and criminal indifference, indifference of most white people in
this country, and their ignorance"—his sense of insecurity was tied to the culture of reserve and to the blindness to the social burdens of people of color
among even well-meaning white people in his community.

Several people related their feelings of insecurity to what they imagined
other people believed about them, a type of questioning and self-doubt that
appeared to be a result of the provisional acceptance mechanism of misrecognition, in which people of color are asked to prove their worthiness of inclusion
over and over again. Frances, a Filipino woman who had lived in her town for
fifteen years, feared that her children were particularly vulnerable to such feelings of insecurity because, unlike her, they had not already built up a lifetime
of assurance about their self-worth: "My children didn't come in with that
self-confidence from the get-go. They see all these blonde girls playing lacrosse

that are like six feet tall, and my daughter is five feet, you know? The younger
people magnify that difference. So, I think that affects them in a different way,
at a base level. It affects their self-esteem." Frances attributed her children's
struggles to fit into their social environment not only to the phenotypic racial
differences they observed between them and their peers but to the contrast
between their insecurity and their white teammates' seeming sense of ease—
ironically, in this case, while participating in an exclusive and expensive sport
that white colonial settlers had originally learned from Indigenous peoples.

In another example of the emotional burden of provisional acceptance,
Julie, a Korean American woman who had been living in her town for five
years, described often feeling discomfited by the stereotypes that some community members, particularly white men, seemed to hold about Asian American women:

> I feel that the way certain men in the community approach me is influ-
> enced by my ethnicity. The way that guy from my church approached me,
> it seemed like he only talked to me because I was Asian. He was in the mil-
> itary in Asia, and he said he is especially interested in Asian people. That
> gave me really weird vibes. Then he made very uncomfortable comments
> about his interactions with Asian women and what kind of racial profiles
> or racial mixes he finds the most attractive.

As these and similar responses reported earlier in this book reveal, people of
color often experienced being judged primarily on the basis of their racial identity rather than on their individual talents or personalities. Such encounters
appeared to perpetuate a cycle in which social distance and provisional acceptance produced feelings of insecurity that in turn often led to self-fulfilling
apprehension about further interactions.

Anxiety

Other interviewees reported experiencing a more extreme emotional symptom that is perhaps best described as anxiety, which they typically explained
as a brooding fear of some contingency or misfortune related to their racial or
ethnic identity. An analysis of those responses indicated that this anxiety was
often prompted by demonstrations of explicit racism, including the growth of

an openly white-nationalist movement and escalating hostility toward racialized minorities at the national level and a number of specific local incidents such as those discussed in earlier chapters. This increased anxiety among people of color in the Upper Valley was demonstrated by Devesh, an Indian man who had lived in his town eleven years. Despite his seeming eagerness to believe that the currently hostile attitude toward immigrants and people of color was a temporary aberration in the political and social status quo of the area, Devesh also worried that it had made his South Asian racial identity more prominent and thereby increased his vulnerability to possible attack:

> I know this community is mature overall, but everyone has their worst-case scenario. Since Trump was elected, [I fear that] my worst-case scenario may be caused by another human living next to me. Five years back, I never worried about that. I thought the people living in this community, maybe ten miles or twenty miles away, they will first of all come and help me. Now, I worry that there are people who may harm me just because I don't look like them.

That even faraway incidents had the power to provoke Devesh's anxiety about his own vulnerability reflects an awareness among many of my respondents that such larger national sentiments are often assimilated into local patterns of thought and action, particularly among members of rural populations that may see themselves as emblematic of "real Americans." The widely reported 2023 violent attack on three young Palestinian Americans not far from the Upper Valley in Burlington, Vermont, later demonstrated that Devesh's fears were not unfounded.

Other residents of color described feeling a kind of free-floating anxiety that did not appear to be directly related to any particular or dramatic encounter with racism but simply the result of a long accumulation of incidents in which they had been misrecognized. For Emma, the negative impacts of explicit racism and provisional acceptance—which in her case included discrimination in hiring, surveillance while out walking with friends, fear of the police during multiple encounters, and being monitored and checked for counterfeit cash in stores—had become so great that she found even the prospect of discussing those experiences anxiety-provoking:

I think it has gotten worse. Even this morning, thinking about doing
this interview, I started feeling anxious. I was thinking, what do I feel
safe talking about and sharing? All these micro-aggressions and macro-
aggressions are carried within me. I have to meditate or do deep breathing.
I have to pull out my tool kit because I know I am getting triggered. Ultimately, I don't feel safe as far as my standing in the community. I have had
an incredibly hard time managing my weight and I know it is stress related.
I am one of those people that, if I feel stressed and I don't feel safe, I hold
onto every calorie that I consume. So, I feel like my health is actually not
good, and I attribute it to my experiences of being a person of color in this
community.

Despite Emma's having cultivated some emotional distance from the racism
she faced, her response demonstrates that the internalized trauma of these experiences was never far from the surface of her emotional life.[5] While echoing Steven's previously reported lack of certainty about where he stands with
people because of the area's culture of supposed colorblindness, Emma explicitly connected that uncertainty to feeling unsafe. Another interviewee, Fei, a
young Chinese American woman who had lived in the Upper Valley for a year
when we spoke, explicitly connected her fear that she might come to harm to a
worry that community members were likely to view her primarily as a member
of a stigmatized racial group rather than as an individual:

I notice my Asianness negatively. Like, if I am perceived in a way because
of my race, I will either be physically unsafe, like verbally assaulted, or
just feel anxious. Really anxious. I was watching Fourth of July fireworks
and, of course, in the whole field of people, I sit next to this one other
Asian family. They were excited and rambunctious and just enjoying the
fireworks. Sitting next to them when they were having fun and being loud
in a way that other people around us weren't made me feel all of a sudden
anxious or just nervous. I was with my partner, who is white, and I was
almost like, "Protect me with your whiteness."

Fei's anxiety in that moment stemmed from an intuition that her racial identity marked her as disruptively foreign in that distinctly American setting.
Lacking a means to differentiate herself from the other non-white group, Fei
felt her only recourse was to align herself with her partner's whiteness.

Others reported feeling anxious because of an immediate threat to their physical safety posed by explicit racism. Chimaobi, a Nigerian man, reported that he had experienced more than one incident of racialized aggression during his two years living in his town, which had left him anxious about the potential for escalation in the future:

> There were two occasions where people yelled at me and used the n-word. Yeah, sometimes when I am walking all alone, especially late at night, I am more disturbed. I hope I won't experience such a thing where it will endanger my life and my safety. I talked about this in my classroom, and some of the students were worried. Yeah, they were worried. They shouted, "What?!" And then my wife, too, she has always wanted me not to walk alone, especially when it is dark. We sort of manifest that sense of fear based on our color. I hope it won't happen to us.

While Chimaobi's worries may not have risen to the level of persistent anxiety, he clearly felt a need to remain vigilant to avoid becoming the target of racial violence. Reporting a similar incident, Katie, an Indonesian woman who had lived in the Upper Valley for more than two decades, had been stunned when someone yelled at her for making an innocent mistake at the grocery store:

> I was doing my grocery and all the lines were open. I went to the closest one without realizing it was for twenty items or less. The cashier was scanning the things, it was almost done, and this lady came and started yelling. I think she assumed I didn't understand English. She started yelling at me, "Can you read the sign?! Can you read the sign?!" Never in my life while living here for twenty-four years has someone treated me like that. I was shocked, and the cashier didn't help.

Katie was surprised both that a stranger could exhibit such unfounded rage and that, despite her more than twenty years in the Upper Valley, she still encountered situations in which she was provisionally accepted. Katie reported that she never returned to that store but instead shopped at a smaller store where "they all know me," demonstrating how misrecognition also works to limit prospects for widespread social integration in the community.

These interviewees' descriptions of the anxiety produced by such repeated reminders of the stigma related to their racial identity support previous research findings that such experiences tend to make their targets ruminate about them and to be more vigilant toward potential threats in their social interactions (Kwate and Meyer 2011). When chronically activated, such anxiety has also been found to have far-reaching physical health consequences (McEwen 1998). Both the emotional toll of the anxiety produced by misrecognition and its potential negative effects on residents' physical health are real-life consequences of the symbolic processes of racial exclusion that take place in culturally white but diversifying rural spaces like the Upper Valley.

Exhaustion

Another emotional consequence of numerous experiences of misrecognition described by respondents of color was exhaustion, which they described as an overall sense of being tired and worn down from their daily interactions with others in the community and a lack of will to exert the energy required to navigate their interactions with white residents. Rimi, a Bengali woman who had lived in her town for thirteen years, described how taxing she found it to manage the feelings of white people while conversing with them, both in general and particularly when the topic of conversation had to do with race: "I feel like I am trying to help them feel comfortable in my company. That is tiring. Sometimes they want to talk about issues that directly matter to me. They have never lived under my skin; they would never know. But we are having these discussions, and I try to make them comfortable." According to Rimi, the effort involved in conforming to white people's conversational expectations included downplaying and minimizing her own feelings, perhaps as a result of an assumption on their part that racism is not a problem in the Upper Valley and that they are not themselves responsible for the harm Rimi often felt. Her reaction can be likened to the burnout often reported by people in caregiving professions in which maintaining cordial relationships is a defining feature of the job. Hayden, a young Black professional who had lived in the Upper Valley for five years, offered another example of conversations related to race that many people of color found particularly wearing:

> I had a guy I knew through church. He invited me to lunch because someone was accusing him of being racist, and he was asking me if I

had ever seen that in him. So, I'm like, "Nah, we've always been cordial. You've never said anything off-putting to me." I didn't know him that well, so I couldn't really speak to that. Mostly, I was just trying to put him at ease because the more I say yes, the more awkward it becomes. So, we are talking, and I have a teammate who comes in who's a Black guy. [The guy I was having lunch with] says "Hello" to him but calls him a different name, and then he turns to me and goes, "Ha-ha, they all look alike, don't they?" It's just like, wow. We just had a whole conversation about me telling you things were cordial and then you say this to me in a joking manner?! That was an awkward situation, but he picked the worst way to fix it. I don't get it, because you would think that when you're talking to a Black guy about not being racist, you don't make racist comments like that.

The beginning of Hayden's story detailed the emotional labor that is often expected of people of color, who find themselves forced to put energy into educating white people and to do so in a non-threatening way so as to put them at ease. The plot twist, in which Hayden's colleague confused his teammate with another Black man and then made an inappropriate racial joke, revealed the exhausting emotional toll not only of having to respond in a measured way to an overtly racist interaction but of recognizing the seeming futility of one's efforts to educate and build bridges across the racial divide.

A number of other people of color I interviewed also described the kind of mental gymnastics involved in determining how they should respond to such experiences of misrecognition as ultimately exhausting. Ayana, for instance, described being drained by the relentless mental exertion of deciding whether a response was warranted, especially given the supposedly colorblind cultural milieu in which she might encounter denial:

That's the constant struggle, right? Do I speak up? And then it's like, if I speak up, am I speaking to deaf ears? Is anything is really going to change? And is speaking up going to exert more energy for myself and make myself even more tired than I already am? When people of color are experiencing these things, and they actually decide to tell you, it is because they actually had the courage to say, "Hey, this happened to me." But I promise you and guarantee you that there are a lot of people within this community— people of color—that have the same exact experiences. But they are just (a) tired, or (b) they know nothing is really going to come of it. Nothing is going to happen, no change is going to be made, so why waste my time in really even putting more effort into this than I already have?

Saima similarly described the continual need to weigh her responses to misrecognition as an emotional burden that she was forced to carry with her every day:

> It stops us from being, living a full life the way everyone else does. It's really difficult, and it's draining. It takes a lot of energy to say, "I'm going to ignore this, I'm going to ignore this." So, by the end of the day it's like, "Phew, I am home, and I can relax and there's no one to judge me." It's not easy. I am going to be very honest. It is not easy. I met some people that are about to buy a house, and I was like, "How? I just need to know how!" And she said she's making it because she has a husband and that's her comfort. My husband is my comfort, too, but I only see him at night. So, it's hard. It's draining.

Saima's story powerfully conveys how everyday efforts to let misrecognition roll off one's back can be so enervating as to make imagining feeling at home in the Upper Valley almost impossible.

Strategies for Coping with Homesickness

A number of the people of color I interviewed discussed the impact of their repeated experiences of misrecognition primarily in terms of particular strategies they had developed to protect their emotional state enough to continue living and working in an environment that often seemed to view them as less fully human than they viewed themselves. Although such stories clearly demonstrated the respondents' own sense of agency by framing themselves as active participants in rather than simply passive victims of the social interactions in which they found themselves, the strategies they had developed also appeared to incur significant emotional costs that make it difficult to define such coping mechanisms as healthy. Indeed, they seem to illustrate what public health scholars have referred to John Henryism, or conditions in which coping strategies have serious physical costs, such as hypertension and cardiovascular disease (Bennett et al. 2004). Furthermore, as the following analysis makes clear, by relying on racialized minority individuals to cope with harm rather than taking action to remediate that harm, these strategies allow the underlying culture of whiteness and its inherent racial hierarchy to remain unaddressed.

Creating an Alternative Community

One such strategy that emerged from the interviewees' responses was forging strong bonds with other marginalized people of color in the area as an alternative method of creating a sense of home within a community that misrecognized their worth. This strategy appeared to have worked well for Visaka, a South Asian woman who for five years had lived in a newly constructed neighborhood in which the residents were more racially and ethnically diverse than those in the rest of the town, thereby allowing her and her neighbors to develop a sort of "village culture" that included often dropping by each other's homes unannounced and providing social support, which Visaka described as having increased her sense of self-assurance in her dealings with the larger Upper Valley community: "I'm becoming more vocal and confident to speak about my heritage and my culture. Before, I would not share, for example, something I grew up eating because people might think I'm weird. But now, I'm like, 'No, this is who I am, and this is how I was raised.'" Similarly, Eswari reported that cultivating ties with a diverse group of friends at work had helped her overcome some of her initial trepidation about living in a predominantly white rural setting: "I feel great because all the [healthcare] fellows are from different places. I'm very close to my friend, who is from Turkey, and she tells me that people always look at her because she wears a hijab. And my other co-fellow is an African American. So, I don't feel alone. I don't feel like it's just me. We can share our experiences." Joining forces with members of other marginalized racial and ethnic groups had helped such residents compensate for the lack of large co-ethnic communities in their rural area by bonding around their shared experiences of exclusion and cultivating a kind of parallel, alternative sense of belonging.

Keeping One's Guard Up

Rather than engaging in strategies for connecting and conversing with others, some interviewees chose to erect social barriers to protect themselves from rejection and the emotional consequences of interacting with the white community. Rimi, for instance, described her decision to close herself off from relationships as a form of protection:

> I now know not to have very much eye contact. Don't smile at random people. You don't need to. You just need to focus; pretend you are busy. I have learned. I avoid situations where I know I might lose control. I don't like it. I mean, I really want to say "Hi," but it's not "mature." It is immaturity if you are showing you are available and happy and ready to talk and mingle and be accepted. I am very afraid to form relationships in this area. You just never know. You have to be very protective of your true self. It is very superficial. And I'm really not very interested in superficial. I am okay. I don't want to open up new relationship accounts. Oh yeah, I have changed—grown thicker skin is what I mean.

Rimi described her evolution over the previous twelve years as metaphorically physiological, as having hardened herself emotionally by developing a sort of shield to protect her from assaults on her humanity. The end result of this strategy, however, was the perpetuation of her social isolation. Describing another defensive strategy, Jocelyn, a Filipina American who had lived in her town for four years, reported that she had learned to arm herself by looking mean when out in public:

> I have perfected the kind of face that shuts that off completely; it's my bus face. Like, I don't smile and I'm not trying to be friendly. I usually look like I don't want anything to do with people. That is something that I have really leaned into over the years. I also have a walk that feels very aggressive and that kind of pushes people away. So, what I have found is that I talk to people who share the same experiences. It is such a unique experience here, trying to fit into a culture and an environment that was created for a specific demographic, where a specific demographic thrives, and people who are not coming from that specific group feel that tension. Trying to explain that to people who have not felt it is more effort than I really want to put into it.

Rimi's developing a thick skin and Jocelyn's using her body like a force field
to repel others are both examples of the kinds of strategies adopted by some
people of color to keep the misrecognition they encounter in their daily interactions from penetrating that surface and hurting them emotionally.

Yet another strategy was demonstrated by Eunice, who reported that she
had chosen to opt out of the mostly white social scene in the Upper Valley and
to instead fulfill her need for connection by traveling frequently to visit friends
in other places:

> I prioritize all my friends that live somewhere else, where I am never sub-
> jected to this kind of stuff. My friends in the Upper Valley are literally 5
> percent of my life. That's how I take care of myself. I have so many other
> friends in other places, and I am very good at keeping in touch with them.
> I don't let these Upper Valley people become such a big part of my life that
> they crowd out everyone else. In fact, I crowd out the Upper Valley expe-
> rience, both by how I travel and by who I focus my time and energy on.

Despite living in the Upper Valley in body, Eunice's mind and heart remained
elsewhere. While such a coping mechanism might effectively diminish the
pain of misrecognition for people of color, it is essentially an avoidance strategy that, by allowing the culture of whiteness in the Upper Valley to go un-
challenged, serves to perpetuate white racial domination and the emotional
toll of misrecognition among other people of color who may not have access to
an alternative community.

Although these various forms of keeping one's guard up can defend people
of color against the everyday emotional harms that may accompany their interactions with their white neighbors, their ultimate impact is to prevent the
formation of deep connections with others in the broader community and
thereby to preclude the possibility of a more racially integrated and equal society within the small towns of the Upper Valley.

Ignoring Misrecognition

A number of other respondents described coping with misrecognition by essentially choosing not to see it as the result of bad intentions in order to not
personalize and internalize racial exclusion. According to Samuel, a Haitian

man who had lived in his town for fifteen years, his key to surviving his life in the Upper Valley was not overthinking others' reactions:

> Of course, for a person of color to come here and make a home, you have to be able to mentally overcome some of the diversity obstacles. Meaning you need to not only be prepared but be deaf as well. Because every time a white person looks at you, whether they look at you funny or happy, you could [assume] it means something . . . that they don't care, or they don't want you to be here. But as soon as you get out of this one, another one will come right back. Then what you're going to do? Accumulate all of them? Then you never get free. And that's what inhibit our lives. This is why we have all kind of disease, all kinds of sickness inside of us. Because of the stuff that we keep holding on and we never let them go. "I'm going to take this to death with me!" That's your choice. Let it eat you. But that's not the solution, you know. If you are living above that, you're cool.

Concluding that he had no control over whether people see him in the way he wanted to be seen and that such misrecognition may be never-ending, Samuel simply chose not to "hear" any negative judgment as a means of being free of the emotional harm that he saw other people of color accumulating.

Shenqing similarly reported choosing not to acknowledge or give much weight to incidents of racial prejudice in the Upper Valley as a strategy for fitting more comfortably into the community. In one such incident, he was attending a hunting show in the area when a stranger passing by him muttered something about "Asians fishing illegally." Although he initially felt hurt by the comment, Shenqing chose not to dwell on it and to instead excuse the person's prejudice as a universal human trait that he could relate to: "It is very common for human beings. Even in China, people in Beijing and Shanghai look down on people from other places. That is understandable. But my thinking is, don't emphasize that too much." Yet neither Shenqing's positive outlook nor the remarkable inroads he had made with the hunting community in the Upper Valley had managed to protect him from being judged as an outsider, illustrating that while the strategy of essentially ignoring racial slights might help people of color maintain their sense of self-worth and protect them from the psychological burden of constantly reacting to incidences of misrecognition, it also ultimately allows white racism and ignorance to proceed largely unchecked.

Other interviewees described efforts they had taken to protect themselves against misrecognition by interpreting and responding to potentially harmful situations in ways that affirmed their own sense of worth and value. Ayana, for example, reported consciously calling upon her cultural background as a Black woman to remind herself that she must see the value in herself because others would not necessarily do so:

> You just realize that people think the way that they think. I don't know why they think like that, or what background they came from. But when you're growing up, especially as a Black woman, you are always told that there are people out there who don't respect you and don't appreciate you, and they don't even know you. It's just because of what you look like and who you hang around. So, growing up and knowing that and being in these situations, it doesn't sting as much. Not to say that it's not wrong, or that people shouldn't talk about it. But you start to care more about change coming versus how you personally feel about it and the pain that you have to withhold from it.

Ayana found that reminding herself that the racism she encountered originated in the cultural environment allowed her not to dwell on the harm it caused in the moment and to instead orient herself toward the future and possibilities for change.

Folade, a Nigerian woman who had lived in her town for two years, reported having learned to protect herself by actively practicing a mindset of unconcern and assuming the best of others whenever possible:

> I try to be indifferent because I feel like people are suffering too much on these racial issues and I don't want to put myself through that. I don't want to suspect anybody's intentions. I don't want to relate to people based on the fact that they are acting weird. I don't want to think about it. I don't want to believe it exists. I know it exists, but I don't want it to constitute a basis for my interaction or my relationship with others. At that moment, I choose not to think about it. My reaction to racial comments and questions is I act the bigger person and make the other person the foolish one. I won't turn it around for you to make me the foolish one. Because when

you argue with them, you cause a rancor, you lose your voice and draw unnecessary attention. And then, people begin to give you a pitiable "Sorry." No, no, no. To avoid all that stuff, I try not to give suspicion to every attitude, every question. I just answer by assuming that you are ignorant. It's your business to choose to be ignorant all your life. I will play the bigger one and the wiser one.

Beyond protecting her from the sting of such interactions, Folade's strategy appeared to allow her to raise her own self-esteem by seeing herself as taking the moral high road relative to her racially insensitive interaction partners.

Saima appeared to have taken such an approach to yet another level by engaging in an explicit strategy of positive self-talk:

In the Upper Valley, these little micro-aggressions are so constant every day of my life because I am around all of these people. I realize that me being happy is very important, and so I have this new exercise now. I tell myself I am going to be happy despite them. Like, "I don't care what happened, I'm going to do this today." I'm not saying I have mastered it, but I'm doing more of it. My husband also reminds me, "Don't give white people your energy!" But it does hurt. Our experiences are dehumanizing.

Nonetheless, Saima's admission of hurt feelings indicates that such efforts to preemptively boost her self-confidence were not enough to fully desensitize her to the misrecognition she experienced. Like the previously identified coping mechanisms, the strategy of ignoring the harm of misrecognition or even of using it as an occasion to affirm one's self-worth is at once an act of empowerment and a form of emotional labor that allows the racialized power relations of the predominantly white community to continue.

Contemplating Leaving

As a result of the cumulative emotional costs of misrecognition, many of the people of color I interviewed had come to doubt whether the Upper Valley would ever really feel like home, and more than half (34 of 58) admitted to having contemplated leaving the Upper Valley to make a future home elsewhere. For some, having that option open seemed to function primarily to ease some of the present sting of homesickness, while others appeared to have already begun to view their time in the Upper Valley as limited.

Some of those who described harboring such thoughts simply could not imagine becoming truly comfortable in a place that offered so little racial and cultural diversity. Hayden, for instance, reported that incidents and disappointments such as his colleague's lack of racial awareness had made him reconsider staying in the Upper Valley:

> Meeting people who were born and raised in Vermont or New Hampshire and who don't have a lot of interactions with people who are diverse from them, that's worst-case scenario. But those sorts of things happen more often than I thought they would. And I have had other people say similar sorts of off-putting things, and again I can tell that they have never done this before. That's where my longing for diversity comes from, that's where not feeling like home comes from. I mean, I'm from Oklahoma, so there's tons of racism back home, it just looks so much different. It's more abrasive: "I know who you are, and I don't like you" sort of deal. I sometimes would much rather people just be abrasive, so we know where we stand, you know?

For Hayden, the particular nexus of the Upper Valley's lack of diversity and the subtle ways in which misrecognition was practiced had made him almost nostalgic for the more overt racism he had grown up with. When I asked Selene, a young Black woman who had lived in the Upper Valley for two years, if she felt at home in her town, she volunteered that the lack of diversity in the area had not only precluded her developing a sense of community but had also filled her with a sense of dread at the thought of raising children in an environment in which they would be treated as racial outsiders:

> No. I will be honest. No, I don't [feel at home]. I hope not to stay here more than two years. It just depends on when the next opportunity will open up. Being a young Black woman in my mid-twenties, what I am looking for is a sense of community. If I was to plant roots, I would have to think about, is this somewhere I want to raise a family? And I think about having children of color and not seeing a lot of people that look like them. I think that could be traumatizing. It is a lot to think about and put into

the equation. Because, you know, there are certain plans you have in your life, and I don't think the Upper Valley would accommodate those for me.

Steven, another interviewee who dismissed making any kind of long-term emotional investment in the Upper Valley, also attributed his intention to eventually leave to the area's overwhelming racial homogeneity:

I know how to navigate this area. I understand this area. I am well-versed in this area. But home? No. Even after seven years, it is unsettling just how pervasively white this community is. So, I wouldn't say that I feel at home. In fact, I think living here has made me feel more like a Southerner because I am definitely not a New Englander. I don't want this to be a long-term place for me. New England, New Hampshire, and specifically [the town where I live], I wouldn't call it home. I would never call it home.

As it had for Hayden, Steven's homesickness had fostered a stronger sense of affiliation with a place where he felt like he belonged—a place with more racial diversity if also a more overt racial hierarchy. Though the Upper Valley is diversifying, the still predominantly white population and culture of the area remained a roadblock that left some interviewees looking for an off ramp.

Others ascribed their thoughts about leaving the Upper Valley more specifically to the difficulty they had encountered in making friends and settling in as acknowledged and welcome members of the community. One such interviewee, Biyu, a young Chinese woman who had lived in her town for ten years, described her ties to the area and its people as tenuous: "We don't rule out the possibility to relocate. We have never objected to relocating because we don't have that many ties here. I wish there is someone I can interact with. Let me rephrase that: right now, the people I work with are just my coworkers. I do not interact with them outside of work. I wish I had someone I can be more closely related to." Seoyun, a Korean professional woman who had lived in her town for seven years, cited a similar lack of closeness in the relationships she had managed to form in the Upper Valley as also making her doubtful about the length of her future there: "Am I going to stay here for my post-retirement years? I don't think so. Even though I have colleagues, I don't say I have any friends. I worry about my post-retirement life. Many people stay here because that's where their friends are. But, for me, I have colleagues but not best friends." Although most of the interviewees seemed to have formed positive professional relationships with the people with whom they worked, comments such as those of Biyu and Seoyun appear to reflect the inherent limitations of such relationships in creating a deeper emotional sense of home. Although most of the interviewees were originally lured to the Upper Valley by professional opportunities, it is possible that the workways and professional culture of the kinds of jobs in which they were employed may have combined with the larger culture of reserve to produce a greater sense of social distance from coworkers than they may have known elsewhere or that might be experienced by other groups of migrants of color.

Many of the interviewees, upon calculating a cost-benefit analysis of staying in the Upper Valley, appeared to have concluded that no career opportunity was worth the emotional costs of misrecognition they found themselves forced to pay. When I interviewed Joseph, a Chinese American who reported having made a concerted effort to build a satisfying life in his town for nine years, he rated his mental health as just fair, an evaluation he linked directly to living in the Upper Valley: "To be honest, I think I would be happier living somewhere else with my kids. I got divorced. I have a fiancé. But I just am not where I thought I would be in life right now. I think that's why, mental health–wise, I'm just not . . . I should be happy with what I have, but I am not happy with where I am." Chimaobi described having similar internal struggles as he attempted to balance his career goals and the emotional costs of living in the Upper Valley: "There are times when I will really want to be calm. When I am experiencing some things, I think, 'Probably time to leave.' I'm going through that sort of decision process where I will question myself, 'Is it worth the time?' This is a very temporary position." Jocelyn, too, grappled with ambivalent feelings about her life in the area that sometimes made her contemplate leaving: "I don't feel negatively toward the Upper Valley, but I don't really feel a close connection to it. It has helped me grow, and I feel like I understand myself better. But it's not necessarily something that I think would continue to feel good. I probably have an expiration date here, honestly." Saima reported that her work as a community organizer had introduced her to many people of color who were so emotionally exhausted by their lives in the Upper Valley that they had eventually made the decision to depart: "It is hard, seeing all these people being drained. They come, stay for a few years, take whatever they need to take from the area, and then leave. Even though we know it is [politically] progressive, even though we know it may not be as harmful as other states, we still leave because it's not healthy for our psyche." Within a year of completing the interview for this study, Saima herself had moved away from the Upper Valley.

Even though the various coping mechanisms described by the interviewees seemed to help them continue to function effectively in their public and professional lives in the Upper Valley, none seemed to entirely protect them from some degree of homesickness. Furthermore, many of those strategies require resources—financial, professional, and personal—that may not be available to other groups of migrants of color and ultimately operate to further deplete their emotional stores and relieve white people of the onus of remediating their own practices and those of their communities.

———

Even though the people of color interviewed for this study had moved to the Upper Valley with great hopes of creating emotionally fulfilling lives for themselves and their families and recounted numerous professional and personal satisfactions related to the lives they had built there, virtually all reported homesickness as a manifestation of the racial demographics and inequality of the region. That those aspirations and the basic human need to be fully seen and accepted had been disappointing for so many, to the point that many had or were considering moving elsewhere, was a loss not only for the interviewees but for the communities and industries into which they had been so actively recruited. But even as the responses analyzed in this chapter powerfully demonstrate the emotional impacts of the exclusionary boundary processes operating within the Upper Valley, they also begin to hint at possibilities for interventions in that situation that would make it more possible for people of color to not only survive but to thrive as equal members in diversifying rural communities in the Upper Valley and elsewhere in the country, which is the topic of the following chapter.

Conclusion

In a 2023 interview (Heilman 2023), John Rodgers, a former Vermont state senator and now lieutenant governor, echoed the previously discussed sentiments of white survey respondents who had suggested that newcomers might successfully develop a sense of being at home in the Upper Valley as long as they did not try to change "our culture." Describing what he saw as differences between the people recently moving to the state and the "Back-to-the-Landers" who had arrived in the 1970s, he declared that those earlier migrants

> came up here and they wanted to be like us. The difference now is a lot of the folks that are coming don't want to be like us. They want to make the Vermont they want. . . . It's only recently that they've started attacking what I feel is our culture of independence—the folks like myself who have firearms and who hunt and fish and trap. . . . I don't care where you came from, you know, what your perspective is, if you can live and let live. What I have a problem with are the people who come here and want to take rights away from us that our families have had for generations, and our foundational rights in our culture.

Even though most of those earlier newcomers had been white and most more recent in-migrants have been people of color, the contrasts Rodgers draws between his working-class identity and the preferences and attitudes of newcomers suggest that class may play at least as much of a role as racial prejudice in the differences he observed. Given that his personal history is so closely bound to the Vermont culture he cherishes, one can sympathize with Rodgers's fear that his way of life is under threat. Nonetheless, the findings of this book suggest that the desire of many longtime Upper Valley residents to simply "live and let live" will not resolve cultural tensions around this newest demographic shift but merely exclude this particular influx of newcomers to the ultimate detriment of not only those newcomers but the community as a whole.

The stories shared in this book demonstrate the multiple ways in which people of color who have chosen to move to the Upper Valley to build a life for themselves and their family and to contribute to the well-being of their new community instead find that they are continually reminded that most of their neighbors view them as less valuable and less worthy of inclusion in the fuller community than longtime white residents. As the data collected from both white and non-white residents suggest, this misrecognition stems from and supports a culture in which longtime Upper Valley residents are able to impose their own interpretation of the way the social life of the region should operate, thereby further hardening the boundaries between an empowered "us" and a marginalized "them." Despite the region's liberal reputation and many residents' insistence that they are not racist, those boundaries serve to maintain a racial hierarchy that has been in place for more than 250 years in Northern New England and to create racialized mental health inequalities even under conditions of relative socioeconomic equality.

What many longtime residents often fail to recognize is that those mental health consequences and the misrecognition from which they stem are a problem not only for people of color hoping to make a home in the Upper Valley but for the populace of the region as a whole. As demographers have pointed out, the rural America that the country has known for at least the last century is literally dying, with outmigration, high mortality, and low fertility producing a downward demographic spiral of rural depopulation that threatens to leave many rural areas unable to maintain critical infrastructure and services and sustain a viable economy for their remaining residents (Johnson 2022). Policymakers at the federal level have attempted to mitigate this demographic crisis with several structural interventions, such as the 2021 American Rescue

Plan Act, which invested in the economic revival of small towns with funding for infrastructure and renewable energy, workforce development, and small business grants. Other programs, such as those intended to alleviate rural healthcare-worker shortages, have introduced a substantial workforce of immigrants of color into rural communities, with the result that those professionals tend be much more racially diverse than the population of the small towns to which they have moved and serve.[1] Although the experiences of a number of the respondents included in this book illustrate that such structural interventions can help attract new residents of color to fill crucial needs in rural communities, they also make clear that such supposed solutions have presented the region with a new and pressing social problem: how to help those individuals of color feel recognized and comfortable enough to actually put down roots and remain in the community.

The insights garnered by this study suggest that enlarging those boundaries will ultimately require longtime residents to move beyond what constitutes an unrealistic and unjust demand that people of color shoulder the burden of assimilating into the existing culture and instead to find ways in which they can actively address and mitigate the impact of misrecognition. To that end, this chapter proposes several strategies that key actors at different levels of the community—from civic and cultural leaders to individual residents—can employ to integrate non-dominant voices, stories, identities, and cultures into community life and narratives. These suggestions reflect a multicultural strategy that, rather than requiring assimilation to the dominant culture or solely positioning racial minorities as recipients of recognition policies, seeks to include people in the collective primarily through broadening the criteria by which individuals and groups can gain cultural membership.[2]

Local Civic Leaders: Affirm and Welcome Diversity

Experiences of communities elsewhere suggest that overcoming the sense of isolation and social distance documented in the previous chapters will require that local civic leaders promote greater recognition of the presence and contributions of residents of color by extending welcoming messages to those residents and communicating that multicultural stance to current residents. A study of systematic group-inclusion efforts by communities across the country found that such efforts—such as local leaders' using informational communication to persuade longtime residents that it is in their interest to join efforts to define their communities as welcoming— helped to break down group boundaries (Okamoto and Ebert 2016). In such an effort intended to stimulate the economy of Rutland, Vermont, just to the west of the Upper Valley, the local government engaged in a branding campaign that invited newcomers, including international refugees and immigrants, to "Live the Life You Were Meant For." Publicly supporting this campaign, leaders of organizations such as the Chamber and Economic Development of the Rutland Region (CEDRR) reminded residents that although the area had "a talented, hardworking labor force," that workforce was also "one that is weighted at the twilight of their careers," and therefore, "to keep our economy strong and growing, we need to grow the available pool of employees" by actively recruiting newcomers (CEDRR 2021). To help garner local support for those efforts, the CEDRR also drew upon narratives of shared values and similar histories that were likely to resonate with longtime residents: "Many of our family histories are a testament to the fact that new arrivals can succeed in the face of obstacles. Provided with opportunity, refugees and immigrants have helped us become the strong Nation and State that we are today. The upcoming planned growth of our community is merely the next logical step in our history of creating opportunity and prosperity for everyone." Despite early public opposition to the resettlement of Syrian refugees in 2016, Rutland has since successfully developed and initiated plans to resettle hundreds of refugees from Afghanistan, and many citizen, faith-based, and business groups have stepped in to assist in those efforts. Part of this apparent turnaround in local sentiment can be attributed to the efforts of local government officials to appeal to shared experiences while endorsing the resettlement plan in public meetings, such as an official reminding attendees at a board of aldermen meeting that "Afghans worked alongside American service members, serving as interpreters, guides, mechanics and more. They often risked their lives and the lives of their families through their allyship" (Cotton 2021).

Beyond disseminating these kinds of direct messages, local governments can also develop and promote inclusive laws and policies intended to destigmatize and support vulnerable populations. For example, in recent years three towns in the Upper Valley passed "welcoming ordinances" that prohibit local police officers from inquiring about individuals' immigration status and sharing any such information with federal authorities. Those measures were intended to protect a marginalized population of color, undocumented immigrants, many of whom are afraid to report crimes or interact with police for fear of having their immigration status uncovered and shared. Passing and enforcing public policies such as those not only provides legal protections to vulnerable residents and workers but also sends a clear message to all residents about who belongs and deserves the community's respect and support.

Yet another way for local civic leaders to foster a broader sense of inclusion and belonging is using public funds to create opportunities in which people with diverse backgrounds can come together in pursuit of common interests. Such efforts might entail allocating resources toward building or strengthening intercultural bonds through neighborhood associations, sports clubs, and charitable associations or hosting multicultural events in inclusive public spaces. Beyond lending logistical and financial support, leaders can encourage multicultural collaboration and visibility in event planning, inviting diverse voices to design or contribute to events in their own ways rather than forcing them to operate within formats or systems that already exist. In rural Iowa, for instance, a local government that had received a federal grant to support a diversity project hired a Latino leader from the local community to plan and implement educational activities focused on reducing misrecognition, such as classes about soccer, culinary traditions, and Latino arts and culture (Sacchetti 2022). The successful experiences of rural officials engaged in such efforts demonstrate the effectiveness of adopting a formal welcoming plan designed to provide strategic guidance and checkpoints toward changing community narratives (Estes 2022).

Cultural Leaders and Knowledge Producers: Tell Inclusive Stories

Local cultural leaders and knowledge producers can also play an important role in reducing misrecognition by employing the arts and cultural activities to help recraft the ways in which the community is imagined by its members. As others have pointed out, aesthetic experiences and arts-based modes of communication provide accessible activities that can mobilize social change by shifting individual perspectives, supporting interaction among groups, and generating shared meanings (Sonke et al. 2019). Such artistic and cultural activities might include free or low-cost performances, exhibits, classes, crafts, and culinary events and can take place in existing venues such as community centers, parks, public streets, theaters, and other public spaces. One particularly inspiring example of a community that has successfully leveraged art to engage in community building is the small town of Tamaqua, Pennsylvania, a former coal-mining town suffering from high levels of opioid addiction and abandoned properties (Engh et al. 2021). In 2011, a Penn State University survey found that the residents of Tamaqua reported the lowest levels of interpersonal and community trust of all the Pennsylvania communities surveyed, with respondents going so far as to declare that there was "nothing worse than life in Tamaqua" and that "the community was doomed." As part of their rejuvenation efforts, the town collaborated with local artists and the nonprofit Center for Community Progress to develop several creative placemaking projects, including "Dear Tamaqua," a year-long letter-writing project that invited residents to share their honest feelings, memories, and perspectives about the town. Intentionally reaching out to residents who "might not feel that their voices are heard or that their opinions matter," the project recruited a team of one hundred volunteer transcribers to gather responses at schools and senior living centers, held events in libraries and on playgrounds, and even distributed coasters printed with the prompt to local bars. As a result, the town received more than seven hundred submissions, which a local arts center used as the source material for a series of arts programs over the next several years, culminating in a 2015 community walking experience in which words and passages from the letters were projected on screens and buildings, and actors and dancers presented performances based on themes that emerged from the letters, all intended to help residents view the community in new ways. Repeating the same survey in 2016, Penn State researchers found significant increases in community connectedness and optimism (Kunkel 2016). As local officials stressed, the success of this arts-based intervention was due in large part to the participatory, safe, and approachable nature of the story collection and artistic expression, which allowed a multitude of views to be shared as representative of the community.

As the Tamaqua example suggests, storytelling is a very powerful strategy that cultural leaders and knowledge workers can employ to change the narrative about who belongs to the collective. By issuing an invitation to view a situation from another's perspective and illuminating points of similarity between people from seemingly different cultures (Lindsey et al. 2015), storytelling can function as a type of symbolic intervention that sociologists call "ordinary cosmopolitanisms," or strategies that enable people to learn about the world in a way that allows them to bridge racial group boundaries (Lamont and Aksartova 2002). As Lamont (2018) notes, one important way in which such knowledge workers and cultural intermediaries as academic and legal experts and social movement leaders and activists can contribute to multicultural efforts is to engage in storytelling about their community on such communication platforms as public television, community radio, print journalism, and social media. Recruiting cultural delegates to share stories representative of the experiences and perspectives of their group can elicit empathy from other members of the community without requiring marginalized people to individually bear the full burden of the emotional labor of interpersonal encounters. In the case of diversifying rural towns, making an array of stories and narratives about the experiences, contributions, and perspectives of a wide range of residents readily available in the public sphere can help foster a more cosmopolitan imagination. One such intervention, based on early findings from the current study, is Humans of the Upper Valley, a campaign that regularly distributes stories from and about a wide range of area residents via social media and email (Walton 2024).

Yet another mode of leveraging the power of storytelling to support multicultural efforts in rural areas is providing opportunities to uncover and share a more inclusive narrative of local history, such as forming a truth-and-reconciliation commission tasked with exposing previously overlooked historical facts and acknowledging past wrongs, such as (as in the case of the Upper Valley) past and present treatment of Indigenous peoples. By creating a record of and raising awareness around historical injustices, such commissions can provide oppressed groups with greater social recognition and some degree of healing from traumatic events. Viewing local history in terms of a longer past may also make it easier for some white residents to recognize and acknowledge contemporary racism within the community and commit to taking steps to combat it, such as eliminating Native-themed school and sports mascots that sustain hurtful stereotypes and various kinds of community commemorations that erase Indigenous presence.[3] Facilitating a broader community understanding of past wrongs can open the door to a wider critique of racist practices and attitudes that is likely to make the Upper Valley and places like it a more comfortable environment for residents of color to work, live, and raise their families.

Individual Residents: Demonstrate Everyday Solidarity

Individual residents also have an important role to play in creating an inclusive, multiculturalist ethos in diversifying rural places. Perhaps the most basic and straightforward way in which white residents can advance those efforts is to commit to learning about how misrecognition works, both in general and in the specific experiences of their neighbors, friends, and coworkers of color. Rather than putting the educational burden on people of color, accepting responsibility for learning about the various forms and impacts of misrecognition might include reading books or articles on the topic on one's own or forming a reading group with other white residents to discuss such works and support each other in gaining greater awareness.[4] As such works and the interview responses in the previous chapters suggest, white residents can also signal to people of color with whom they have close and trusting relationships that they are open to talking honestly and respectfully about race. If a person of color shares a racialized observation or a hurtful experience he or she had within the community, a good first reaction is to listen with openness and curiosity rather than excusing such incidents as the result of innocent intentions or denying that they were race-related. Such firsthand learning about the experiences of people of color with whom one is acquainted can both help longtime residents better understand how their community is experienced by such newcomers and help those newcomers feel more truly seen and heard.

Gaining such an understanding of the ways in which misrecognition operates in their communities can also help white residents recognize when and in what ways they might take specific actions to intervene on behalf of people of color and more-inclusive social relations. As critical race scholars argue, an important way in which individual citizens can advance racial equity in their communities is to commit to being not simply non-racist but consciously anti-racist, which involves identifying and opposing racism in one's daily life.[5]

Ways in which individual white residents can practice anti-racism might include putting their learning into practice by speaking up when observing misrecognition in their social and professional situations and participating in and demonstrating support for community activities such as those recommended above that can broaden the cultural horizons of the residents of their small towns. As Lamont (2018) argues, even participation in such relatively low-stakes social justice activities as displaying visual symbols such as rainbow flags and welcoming lawn signs like those stating "No matter where you are from, we're glad you're our neighbor" can contribute to a broader definition of collective identity and help dissolve group boundaries within communities. Although it can take courage to publicly proclaim one's beliefs, especially if they differ from those most commonly expressed within one's community, doing so can serve as a catalyst to encourage others to also demonstrate multicultural awareness. By taking such actions, individual residents of rural areas like the Upper Valley can help make their communities places in which people of color feel sufficiently recognized and comfortable to commit to putting down roots and making that space their home.

———

"Live and Let Live." "Live Free or Die." "Don't Tread on Me." Despite the illustrious historical pedigree and wide acceptance of such tenets among residents of Northern New England, the findings of this study suggest that they too often serve to justify inaction, indifference, and nonintervention in the prevailing social and cultural status quo of the region and to exclude people of color from the socially constructed definition of who belongs to the community. People in such diversifying rural areas as the Upper Valley thus face a choice: they can do nothing and thereby effectively reinforce the white cultural status quo, or they can take action to broaden the scope of "who we are" beyond "who we have always been." Rather than passively accepting or mourning the demographic changes taking place in their community, long-time residents ultimately have the most to gain by taking positive action to transform rural places into equitable environments in which people of all racial and ethnic identities are seen and valued for who they actually are and what they have to contribute to the present and future flourishing of their new homes.

Methodological Appendix

The findings in this book are based on a qualitative analysis of interview, survey, participant observation, and secondary source data collected in the Upper Valley primarily between March 2018 and May 2024. Given that my identity as a white woman interviewing non-white individuals about their experiences in a predominantly white space introduced a power imbalance into the research, I actively worked to remain cognizant and thoughtful regarding my racial status in my questions, interactions with interviewees, and interpretations of the data. I aimed not to presume my own expertise and I privileged participants' experiences and understandings over my own. My research team comprised students from an array of backgrounds—Vietnamese American, Chinese American, Korean American, Brazilian, Latina, multiracial, white, and Black—and participated in countless analytic discussions about our interactions in the field. Nonetheless, I acknowledge that the analyses are interpreted through a white lens and urge readers to keep that in mind.

The research assistants and I interviewed N=58 non-white individuals living in the Upper Valley. I used my professional and social networks to initiate the recruitment of participants with a convenience sample and expanded that recruitment through snowball sampling. As discussed below and shown in table A.1, this resulted in a sample that was composed of a plurality of Asian and Asian American individuals, followed by a substantial representation of US-born Black and Caribbean Black individuals but just a few Latino immigrants, African immigrants, and Native Americans. The interview sample included just one US-born Latino and one US-born and one immigrant Middle Eastern individual. The median age of participants was forty-two years old, and their median time living in the Upper Valley was seven years. The sample was 53% female, and 79% of the participants had a professional occupational status, defined as working in a job that required a college or advanced degree.

Although the plurality of Asian Americans and Asian immigrants in the sample is quite different from the populations studied in the existing literature on rurality, race, and incorporation, I consider this feature a strength of this study, as it allowed me to utilize a framework that examines both the processes of racism and immigrant incorporation. At the same time, that US-born and immigrant Asians constitute 62% of the sample is greater than their actual presence in Upper Valley, where they make up 41% of the non-white population, while US-born and immigrant Latino individuals make up only 7% of the study sample but represent 27% of the non-white population in the Upper Valley. Part of this oversampling of Asian and Asian American individuals reflects my relying on a convenience sample in the early stages of data collection, and the lack of Latino representation reflects the somewhat elusive nature of the Latino population in the Upper Valley, among whom I had a harder time gaining acceptance and interest in participating in the study. While the preponderance of immigrants in the sample can be partially explained by the fact that 71% of all Asian American adults in the United States were born in another country, it also reflects that the Upper Valley employment context is dominated by education, healthcare, and technology sectors that often recruit from a global workforce and capitalize on US immigration policies that favor highly educated workers. The analyses presented in this book focus on themes that were widely represented in the data and include quotations that captured these themes across many racial and nativity groups.

The interviews with participants were semi-structured, with most lasting approximately an hour; the shortest lasted twenty-nine minutes and the longest one hour and twenty-six minutes. Interviews were always conducted at a location of the participant's choosing (most often their house or a café), and participants were given a $25 incentive for participation. The interview ques-

TABLE A.1. Selected sociodemographic characteristics among interviewees of color (N=58).

Race and nativity	Participants	Percent	Median age	Median years UV	Female	Professional
Asian immigrant	29	50.0%	42	10	18	24
Asian American	7	12.1%	45	4	4	7
US-born Black	8	13.8%	32	4	4	8
Caribbean Black	4	6.9%	48	3.5	1	2
Latino immigrant	3	5.2%	50	9	1	2
African immigrant	2	3.4%	45	4.1	1	1
Native American	2	3.4%	35	11	1	1
Middle Eastern immigrant	1	1.7%	52	16	0	1
Middle Eastern American	1	1.7%	42	2	1	0
US-born Latino	1	1.7%	31	18	0	0
Total sample	58	100.0%	42	7	53.0%	79.0%

Source: author's interview data.

tions were focused on gathering participants' impressions of the local community; perspectives on knowing others and being known; feelings about and definitions of home, local attachment and participation; sociodemographic questions; experiences with race and stereotypes; health and mental health; and personal worries.

A qualitative-research approach such as that employed in this study is recognized as effective for eliciting the meaning of personal and cultural phenomena and understanding the nature of processes that may help generate and refine social theory (Small 2009). I allowed themes and concepts that emerged from the data—such as feelings of value and respect, seeing oneself represented, disengaging, performance, and demeaning treatment—to drive my ongoing analyses, developing interview questions to pursue certain lines of inquiry throughout the course of the study (Charmaz 2006). I applied case study logic to the sampling procedures (Yin 2009), wherein each case provided an increasingly accurate understanding of the questions at hand and informed the next case. I used Atlas.ti to perform open and then focused coding as key themes related to cultural context, misrecognition, and mental well-being emerged throughout the data collection, analysis, and writing processes. In particular, I did not approach the data collection with misrecognition in mind as a theoretical concept, but rather developed interview questions using a theoretical framework pertaining to belonging and social boundary processes and a social-determinants-of-health focus on well-being. As my findings on structure, culture, misrecognition, and mental health emerged, I came to the data with known theories, using an abductive approach (Timmermans and Tavory 2012) to create some preliminary theoretical explanations and coded the data a second time focusing on detailing the mechanisms. Ultimately, I developed the conceptual model that related and integrated my larger categories, as represented in figure 0.1.

The survey data regarding white respondents was collected by a community-based survey mailed to a randomized sample of 700 residents living in four towns—Lebanon and Claremont in New Hampshire and Hartford and Hartland in Vermont—which are both different from each other and roughly representative of the towns within the Upper Valley, with populations ranging from approximately 350 to 13,500 and varied socioeconomic profiles. I purchased address data from DirectMail.com, a marketing company that compiles lists of verified addresses and names for direct-to-consumer advertising. Using a random number generator, I selected 200 individuals from each of the three larger towns (all over 10,000 population) and 100 individuals from the smaller town (Hartland, VT) to receive mail surveys. Each survey respondent received a $25 visa gift card to thank them for their time.

I received 187 responses out of 700 surveys sent, a response rate of 27%. Of the 187 completed surveys, 162 (87%) were submitted by individuals who identified themselves as white and US-born. Of those 162, I utilized data from 147 white, US-born respondents who submitted complete data on the survey questions of interest for the analyses presented in chapters 1 and 2. As shown in table A.2, a majority of those respondents were male (59%) and a plurality were middle-aged (47% were between thirty-six and sixty-five years old). Only 12% of the respondents reported a family income above $150,000, although 32% held a professional educational degree. Nearly a third (32%) of the respondents were unemployed, demonstrating the wide variation in the socioeconomic profiles of area residents. Respondents reported having lived in their town for a range of one to ninety-three years, with the median length of residency being twenty-two years.

Though the survey included many questions, the analyses in this book utilized the responses to only a few, as described within the chapters in which they are discussed.

TABLE A.2. Selected sociodemographic characteristics among white survey respondents (N=147).

	Total	Percent
Gender		
Female	60	40.8%
Male	87	59.2%
Age		
20-35 years	21	14.3%
36-65 years	69	46.9%
66+ years	57	38.8%
Median family income		
Less than $20,000	5	3.4%
$20,000-49,000	44	29.9%
$50,000-84,000	39	26.5%
$85,000-149,999	42	28.6%
$150,000 +	17	11.6%
Educational attainment		
Less than high school	1	0.7%
High school or GED	26	17.7%
Some college	28	19.0%
College	45	30.6%
Professional degree	47	32.0%
Employment status		
Unemployed	47	32.0%
Employed	100	68.0%
Years lived in town		
Min	1	
Max	93	
Median	22	
Multigenerational resident	N=10	6.8%

Source: author's survey data.

Notes

Introduction

1. Colleges and hospitals are large private employers that are often referred to as anchor institutions because they are physically embedded in place, unlike corporate headquarters or sports teams that are more likely to relocate to follow financial incentives. They also tend to be durable through economic recessions, to employ a large labor force, and, in recognition that their fates are tied to those of the places in which they are located, to often invest in community stability efforts (Harkavy and Zuckerman 1999).

2. While the area has also attracted some low-income Latino labor migrants whose expertise and care have played an important role in sustaining the area's dairy industry, their contribution to racial change in the Upper Valley has remained relatively modest and less visible. A number of Dartmouth College faculty and students have attempted to raise public awareness of the plight of migrant farmworkers in the Upper Valley, who struggle with long hours and difficult working conditions, need assistance with medical bills, and often fear going out in public. See, for instance, Nelson (2020).

3. For example, longtime working-class residents of rural Washington's "Paradise Valley" have felt themselves being marginalized and culturally disenfranchised as the economy shifts toward amenity-based tourism (Sherman 2018). In rural Pennsylvania's Marcellus Shale region, working-class residents have been largely excluded from the job growth and economic expansion accompanying nat-

ural resource development in the area (Schafft 2018). A study of a rural Northern California community that experienced an influx of wealthier and more highly educated newcomers reports that old-timers have found their moral capital a less valuable currency than newcomers' human capital (Sherman 2006).

4. The rural white population of the US declined from 48 million to 34.5 million between 1980 and 2020, while the non-white population grew from 7.7 million to 10.8 million during that time period (Lichter and Johnson 2023).

5. As Danbold and Huo (2015) argue, racial and ethnic diversification challenges the automaticity of white claims to social citizenship based on shared language, values, and an inherited multigenerational claim to the land. Neal et al. (2013) refer to these diversifying communities as "places in process," which captures the sense of uncertainty many residents feel as they negotiate demographic and cultural complexity in their daily interactions. Some white communities have framed the racial changes they have observed as a siege, imagining themselves living in "invaded territory" (Jaworsky et al. 2012) and viewing people of color as "trespassing" on their land (Lung-Amam 2017). Historically, waves of non-white migration and immigration have been accompanied by increases in nativism and xenophobia. In fact, much of today's white power movement publicly draws upon replacement theory, a system of thought originally conceived by French nationalists and eugenicists in the early twentieth century, to argue that white people are literally being replaced by undeserving outsiders (e.g., immigrants and people of color). This notion was found to motivate many who participated in the January 6, 2021, insurrection at the US Capitol Building, among whom those most likely to be charged came from counties with the steepest declines in the proportion of white people in their populations (Pape 2022).

6. Social scientists understand the implicit mental appraisal of one's own social status relative to that of others as a cultural process of recognition in which we determine who matters, who is seen, who is afforded dignity, and who has a seat at the table (Lamont 2023). As cultural scholars have noted, making these distinctions about the value and worth of others is a critical mechanism through which dominant individuals can maintain symbolic power with their group (Bourdieu 1987; Lamont and Molnár 2002).

Chapter 1

1. As anthropologist Elizabeth Carpenter-Song (2023) has observed, the visible wealth of the many high-income and highly educated workers tends to obscure a major housing crisis in Upper Valley communities, in which many residents with low-income, service-sector jobs cannot afford market-value rent in the area.

2. Following King George III's declaration nearly three centuries ago that the

river belonged to New Hampshire, the legal boundary between the two states currently lies at the river's mean low-water mark on the Vermont side (Driehaus 2023). Although the river geographically divides the Upper Valley area into two states, in practice, as Christina Tree (2014) reports in the *Yankee Magazine*, the river operates as "more of a bond than a boundary."

3. One resident, for instance, commented, "I've always thought of the 'Upper Valley' as more of a feeling than a science; therefore, my choices . . . are as difficult to explain as melancholy or joy." Others appeared to base their sense of geographic boundaries on their felt connection to place, such as what one described as their sense of "innate familiarity—anything beyond this boundary is a place where I . . . would feel like a stranger."

4. Note that Figure 1.1 depicts percentage rather than numerical changes in white and non-white populations and that, given that the non-white populations were so small to begin with, even small changes in actual numbers can yield a large change in percentage. Despite the differences in the baseline population counts of the two groups, the figure usefully reveals trends in racial population growth and decline.

5. As one researcher noted, even though the white population of rural areas of the US still averaged 80 percent as of 2012, 82 percent of the population growth in those areas during 2000–2010 took place among people of color (Lichter 2012).

6. Historical information about the city of Claremont comes from City of Claremont 2024.

7. To protect the confidentiality of the interviewees, no identifying personal details are included in these discussions of the towns in which they live.

8. In the early 1800s, when many of the forested areas around Hanover were cleared and burned for pastures, it was customary for local animals to be brought to the Green to graze overnight. In 1836 in response to students' complaints about the "unpleasantness under foot" on their athletic fields and a protest in which cattle were herded into the basement of Dartmouth Hall, the Green was fenced off, but it is still used by town residents for recreation and holiday celebrations. Today, it is not clear whether the Town of Hanover or Dartmouth College owns the Green. The historical information about the Town of Hanover comes from a variety of sources, including Hanover Historical Society 2024, Wikipedia 2024, and Rauner Special Collections Library 2015.

9. In metro areas, policymakers are increasingly looking toward such "eds and meds" institutions as potential drivers of economic development, but these institutions are still uncommon in rural areas.

10. This historical information comes from a variety of sources, including Town of Hartford 2024, Hartford VT Historical Society 2024, and Derkacz 2009.

11. These five villages are Quechee, White River Junction, Hartford, West Hartford, and Wilder. Because the designated villages for which census data are available are not consistent over time, I aggregated the data from two villages— White River Junction and Wilder—into a single area comprising a well-defined downtown and surrounding neighborhoods.

12. As a result of the ongoing process of socioeconomic change in Hartford, media reports on longtime residents' feelings indicate many seem to view it as a strange brew of old and new, which in turn appears to produce some economic and social tension. In a radio interview, for instance, one white resident who had lived for sixty-five years on a street that "was all my relatives at one time" lamented that he "can't afford to patronize the newer businesses in town" and that "the affordability for housing in this town is terrible, especially for low-income folks like myself at this point in my life" (Evancie 2022). Although the speaker did not specifically refer to the race of the higher-income residents implicated in these changes, that so many of those newcomers to Hartford (as in most of the towns in the Upper Valley) were noticeably non-white appeared to create a situation ripe for racial resentment, as will be demonstrated in later analyses.

Chapter 2

1. In response to such concerns, the Vermont governor had enacted severe travel restrictions that discouraged nonresidents from even entering the state, going so far as to pay transportation workers to park at the borders to monitor the quantity of out-of-state license plates. Such restrictions lent an air of legitimacy to a long-standing regional culture of disdain for outsiders, or "flatlanders," as Northern New Englanders often refer to folks deemed "not from around here."

2. As others have noted, rural Northern New England culture is steeped in a long history of forgetting what Doane has described as a narrative of "settler indigeneity" in which English settlers are depicted as the first "civilized" inhabitants of the land and that accordingly serves as a basis for a claim to the "real American" identity (2021, 2). Those two centuries of supposed white racial isolation contributed to what Bonilla-Silva has termed a strong white habitus, the product of an "uninterrupted socialization process that conditions and creates whites' racial taste, perceptions, feelings, and emotions and their views on racial matters" and renders those predilections essentially invisible to most white residents (2018, 121). Furthermore, such privileging of white culture is not overtly stated but simply assumed in what Bhopal has described as "white spaces that are not neatly framed by a sign stating 'Whites only'" (2023, 115).

3. As classical social theory posits, such cultural attitudes and practices strengthen the internal bonds among members of a community and thus are an

important basis for social solidarity (Durkheim 1965 [1912]). Although the culture of a given place can, if unrecognized by those who practice it, act to reproduce inequality, it is also a social construct that is "interpreted, narrated, perceived, felt, understood, and imagined" (Gieryn 2000, 465) by residents of places and thus can theoretically be flexible and malleable over time to reflect changes in the people who live there.

4. White survey participants provided written responses to these questions on a paper survey form. The responses quoted here and elsewhere in the book retain their original wording, spelling, and punctuation.

5. Responses that were reclassified included such obvious instances as "more ethnic folks live here than before" and "definitely more non-white population than when we moved here" as well as reports of having noticed such changes but thinking that others may not be aware of them, such as "[about] 40% of my class-mates were partly Native, but not acknowledged as such. I'm 1st generation Pole, but I, like my contemporaries worked hard not to stand out." A few other respondents admitted to observing racial changes but appeared eager to distinguish such observations from racism, with comments such as "I have noticed an increase but not an increase of becoming racist! I am kind of beyond mind blown how this nation has turned out, racism needs to stop!" and "in the past 5 or so years, more racial people have lived in this town. I treat them with respect as well as they do me. I feel they are not taking any jobs away from anyone." It should also be noted that thirty of these white respondents (a majority of whom lived in Hartford, VT) had lived in the Upper Valley for less than five years themselves, which may not have been enough time for them to notice significant racial and ethnic change in their communities.

6. Sociological research has demonstrated ways in which rhetorical discourses and public perceptions about immigrant criminality have been used to construct social boundaries that render Latino immigrants unsuitable for incorporation into the national identity (Sohoni and Sohoni 2014). Health researchers have also noted stigmas that often accompany people of color migrating from cities to more rural areas, where Black Americans in particular are perceived to be culturally pre-disposed toward poverty (Keene and Padilla 2014).

7. Cheekily summarizing these sentiments in a series of essays, Noel Perrin, a former Dartmouth English professor and Upper Valley resident, suggested that newcomers should adapt to rural life by "raising pigs, growing vegetables, cutting their own firewood and volunteering at church suppers" and be required to plead their "immigration" case before a board "composed entirely of native farmers, loggers, and road-crew men" (Perrin 1980).

8. The general tendency among survey takers to want to present a positive im-

pression of themselves, which social scientists refer to as a social desirability response bias, is widely thought to underestimate the actual existence of prejudice
among such participants, meaning that this percentage might still be assumed to
be a somewhat conservative one.

9. As Kendi (2020) has pointed out and such responses demonstrate, *freedom*
tends to mean different things to different groups in the US: whereas communities
of color have historically sought *freedom from* disenfranchisement, exploitation,
poverty, and injustice, white people have enjoyed nearly unlimited *freedom to* in-
flict those conditions on non-white people.

10. In a recent example of the symbolic importance of the flag to many residents of the Upper Valley, a select-board member from the town of Hartford who
questioned whether the town should continue its practice of flying the American
flag in more than two dozen places—stating in a public meeting that the "flag is
not necessarily a symbol that everyone relates to and admires"—was subjected to
severe backlash on local social media, including suggestions by some residents that
she should move elsewhere if she felt that way (Kenyon 2022).

11. The rise of the MAGA movement since 2016 has led to an increase in people
claiming that the US is a republic rather than a democracy, a rhetorical move away
from democracy that appears to serve a conservative political strategy for maintaining white dominance despite declines in the number of white voters. Docu-
mentarian Astra Taylor, for instance, found that most of the people she talked to
on the street who espoused this rhetoric tended to be white men, who, "looking
back on the sweep of American history, see themselves as safely at the center of the
narrative, and typically they see their present privileges under threat" (Keating
2020).

Chapter 3

1. For more on recognition, see Appiah 1994; Fraser 2000; Lamont 2018, 2023;
Taylor 1994.

2. As previous research has shown, white people often deploy controlling
images that characterize Black men as having lower-class and aggressive characteristics (Meghji 2018).

3. See, for example, news stories about eight school mascots in Vermont (D'Auria 2023) and the New Hampshire legislature's rejection of a measure seeking to
ban the use of Native American symbols and mascots (Rogers 2022).

4. Greg explained that he chose to identify as Native American in order to put
other people at ease: "I got the phenotype from my mom. It seems easier to associate that way when I answer the questions 'Why do you look the way you look?',
'How did you turn out Brown?' It's easier to say, 'Well, I'm Native American.' So,

I guess if I can't pass as standard white guy even though I'm genetically fairly similar, you know, that's probably a big reason. It wasn't culturally a huge part of my life. I didn't even know I was Native American when I was a kid. But I guess there was always that aspect of understanding why I'm different. It fits what people need to understand about me."

Chapter 4

1. As other scholars have noted, home is not simply a physical space but an emotional one associated with feelings of haven, refuge, privacy, and comfort (Ahmed 1999; Fried 2000; Tucker 1994). Without a secure and enduring sense of home, one may feel tenuously and conditionally accepted, which makes the ability to achieve home fundamental to the project of belonging and membership in community. Whereas white people's historical predominance in Northern New England allows them to make confident and uncontested claims to home, racialized others have most often been seen as illegitimate and out of place.

2. These questions included who they discuss personal worries or important decisions with, whether they feel valued and at home in their community, what they would change about their community if they could, and whether they feel attached to and see themselves staying in their community in the long term. This finding regarding the primary source of homesickness is consistent with a large body of scholarship that has demonstrated multiple ways in which race-related stressors, such as discrimination or hostility, can negatively affect the mental health of racial and ethnic minorities (e.g., Williams 2018).

3. Social psychologists have long suggested that social interaction acts as a mirror or looking glass, with the result that one's sense of self and self-esteem tends to depend upon others' impressions of one's worth (Cooley 1902). In *The Souls of Black Folk*, W. E. B. Du Bois famously described others' negative valuations of racial and ethnic minorities as producing "a peculiar sensation, this double-consciousness, this sense of always looking at one's self through the eyes of others, of measuring one's soul by the tape of a world that looks on in amused contempt and pity" (1986 [1903], 364).

4. Answers to this validated self-rated mental health question have been shown to correlate with an array of mental morbidity measures corresponding to psychological distress and with both self-reported and DSM-diagnosed mental disorders. Subjective perceptions of emotional well-being are also important in their own right, as they measure the extent to which individuals are satisfied with their mental health and their ability to perform their usual activities, regardless of whether they have received an official diagnosis of a mental disorder.

5. The feelings described by Emma seem to support recent calls by Monnica

Williams and colleagues (2021) to legitimize the clinical category of racial trauma, defined as "the cumulative traumatizing impact of racism on a racialized individual, which can include individual acts of racial discrimination combined with systemic racism," because it contributes to post-traumatic stress disorder (PTSD).

Conclusion

1. Employers in the Upper Valley have historically had difficulty retaining employees of color, a difficulty that the CEO of Dartmouth Health has attributed primarily to structural factors endemic to rural areas, such as limited housing and public transportation (Doyle-Burr 2018).

2. Scholars of multiculturalism have argued that solely positioning racial minority identities as the recipients of recognition policies (e.g., as some have argued the Black Lives Matter movement does) may induce feelings of threat and siege among white people, thereby shutting down understanding of commonalities and further hardening boundaries between groups (Martineau 2012; Parekh 2005).

3. As Post and Rhodes (2022) note, Indigenous peoples have played a vital role in "reframing and reclaiming" public spaces around the country, particularly through reasserting Native place names on street signs and playing a prominent role in revising the history displayed to the public on markers and commemorative sites.

4. Within the expansive literature on anti-racism and creating more equitable communities, Michèle Lamont's (2023) book, *Seeing Others: How Recognition Works—And How It Can Heal a Divided World*, is an accessible and compelling overview of forty years of her research on the topic.

5. Describing the difference between being non-racist and being anti-racist, sociologist and activist Eduardo Bonilla-Silva writes, "Whereas liberals feel bad when a person of color is murdered by the police, the anti-racist agitates, organizes, and works with every ounce of her soul to eliminate the system that makes possible racialized policing in the first place" (2018, 243). Being an anti-racist means becoming attuned to how racial hierarchy and power undergird social interactions between white people and people of color. Practicing anti-racism means understanding that making a mistake does not make one a bad person, but it does make one responsible for committing to do better next time.

References

Ahmed, Sarah. 1999. "Home and Away: Narratives of Migration and Estrangement." *International Journal of Cultural Studies* 2 (3): 329–347.

Anderson, Elijah. 2015. "The White Space." *Sociology of Race & Ethnicity* 1 (1): 10–21.

Appiah, Kwame A. 1994. "Identity, Authenticity, Survival: Multicultural Societies and Social Reproduction." In *Multiculturalism: Examining the Politics of Recognition, edited by Amy Guttman*, 149–163. Princeton: Princeton University Press.

Bennett, Gary G., Marcellus M. Merritt, John J. Sollers III, Christopher L. Edwards, Keith E. Whitfield, Dwayne T. Brandon, and Reginald D. Tucker. 2004. "Stress, Coping, and Health Outcomes Among African-Americans: A Review of the John Henryism Hypothesis." *Psychology & Health* 19 (3): 369–383.

Bhopal, Kalwant. 2023. "Critical Race Theory: Confronting, Challenging, and Rethinking White Privilege." *Annual Review of Sociology* 49: 111–128.

Big 7 Travel. 2019. "The 50 Friendliest States in America." https://bigseventravel.com/2019/08/the-50-friendliest-states-in-america/.

Blumer, Herbert. 1958. "Race Prejudice as a Sense of Group Position." *The Pacific Sociological Review* 1 (1): 3–7.

Bonilla-Silva, Eduardo. 2018. *Racism Without Racists: Color-Blind Racism and the Persistence of Racial Inequality in America*. Lanham, MD: Rowman & Littlefield.

Bourdieu, Pierre. 1987. "What Makes a Social Class? On the Theoretical and Practical Existence of Groups." *Berkeley Journal of Sociology* 32: 1–18.

Brenan, Megan. 2022. "Americans' Reported Mental Health at New Low; More Seek Help." Gallup, "News." https://news.gallup.com/poll/467303/americans-reported-mental-health-new-low-seek-help.aspx.

Carpenter-Song, Elizabeth. 2023. *Families on the Edge: Experiences of Homelessness and Care in Rural New England*. Cambridge, MA: The MIT Press.

Carr, Patrick J., and Maria J. Kefalas. 2009. *Hollowing Out the Middle: The Rural Brain Drain and What It Means for America*. Boston: Beacon Press.

Chamber & Economic Development of the Rutland Region (CEDRR). 2021. "Statement from the Chamber & Economic Development of the Rutland Region on Refugee Resettlement." September 8. https://rutlandvermont.com/statement-from-the-chamber-economic-development-of-the-rutland-region-on-refugee-resettlement/.

Charmaz, Kathy. 2006. *Constructing Grounded Theory: A Practical Guide Through Qualitative Analysis*. Thousand Oaks, CA: Sage.

Chiumenti, Nicholas. 2020. *Recent Trends in Residential Segregation in New England*. New England Public Policy Center, April 8.

City of Claremont. 2024. "History." https://www.claremontnh.com/history.

Cooley, Charles Horton. 1902. *Human Nature and the Social Order*. New York: Charles Scribner's Sons.

Cotton, Emma. 2021. "Officials Express Broad Support for Afghan Refugee Resettlement in Rutland." *VT Digger*, September 8.

Cousineau, Michael. 2022. "Claremont: Signs of Success on a Long Road to Revival." *New Hampshire Union Leader*, April 3.

Danbold, Felix, and Yuen J. Huo. 2015. "No Longer 'All-American'? Whites' Defensive Reactions to Their Numerical Decline." *Social Psychological and Personality Science* 6 (2): 210–218.

D'Auria, Peter. 2023. "Vermont Equity Organizations Seek to Retire 8 School Mascots." *VT Digger*, February 20.

Derkacz, Scott. 2009. "The Town of Hartford Agricultural Narrative." https://www.uvm.edu/~hp206/2009/Hartford/Hartford%20Agricultural%20History.htm.

Doane, Ashley (Woody). 2021. "From the "Beginning": Anglo-American Settler Colonialism in New England." *Genealogy* 5 (97): 1–23.

Doyle-Burr, Nora. 2018. "Dartmouth-Hitchcock CEO: Region Needs Health Workers." *Valley News*, January 17.

Driehaus, Alex. 2023. "NH, Vermont Meet in Upper Valley to Agree on Border." *Valley News*, October 6.

Du Bois, W. E. B. 1986 [1903]. *The Souls of Black Folk*. In *W. E. B. Du Bois: Writings*, edited by Nathan Huggins. New York: The Library of America.

Dupuis, Ann, and David C. Thorns. 1998. "Home, Home Ownership and the Search for Ontological Security." *The Sociological Review* 46 (1): 24–47.

Durkheim, Émile. 1965 [1912]. *The Elementary Forms of Religious Life*. New York: The Free Press.

Ehrkamp, Patricia, and Caroline Nagel. 2014. "'Under the Radar': Undocumented Immigrants, Christian Faith Communities, and the Precarious Spaces of Welcome in the U.S. South." *Annals of the Association of American Geographers* 104 (2): 319–328.

Embrick, David G., and Wendy Leo Moore. 2020. "White Space(s) and the Reproduction of White Supremacy." *American Behavioral Scientist* 64 (14): 1935–1945.

Engh, Rachel, Ben Martin, Susannah Laramee Kidd, and Anne Gadwa Nicodemus. 2021. *WE-making: How Arts & Culture Unite People to Work Toward Community Well-Being*. Easton, PA: Metris Arts Consulting.

Estes, Chris. 2022. "Ensuring Rural Communities Welcome Everyone." *Community Strategies Group* (blog). Aspen Institute, December 13. https://www.aspencsg.org/ensuring-rural-communities-welcome-everyone-2/.

Evancie, Angela. 2022. "What's the Secret to Downtown Revitalization? Ask White River Junction." *Vermont Public*, October 6.

Fraser, Nancy. 2000. "Rethinking Recognition." *New Left Review* 3: 107–120.

Fried, Marc. 2000. "Continuities and Discontinuities of Place." *Journal of Environmental Psychology* 20: 193–205.

Giddens, Anthony. 1991. *Modernity and Self-Identity: Self and Society in the Late Modern Age*. Stanford, CA: Stanford University Press.

Gieryn, Thomas F. 2000. "A Space for Place in Sociology." *Annual Review of Sociology* 26: 463–496.

Guerra, Cristela, and Travis Andersen. 2017. "After Alleged Taunting and Hanging, N.H. Town Comes Together." *The Boston Globe*, September 12.

Hanover Historical Society. 2024. "Timeline of Hanover, New Hampshire History." https://hanoverhistory.org/timeline-of-hanover-new-hampshire-history/.

Harkavy, Ira, and Harmon Zuckerman. 1999. *Eds and Meds: Cities' Hidden Assets*. Washington, DC: The Brookings Institution, September 1.

Hartford, VT Historical Society. 2024. "Hartford's Story Started in 1761." https://hartfordvthistory.com/.

Hauser, Christine, and Katharine Q. Seelye. 2017. "New Hampshire Investigates Wounding of 8-Year-Old as Possible Hate Crime." *The New York Times*, September 13.

Heilman, Erica. 2023. "West Glover's John Rodgers on Why There Are So Few Working Class People in the Vt. Legislature." *Vermont Public*, April 27, 2023.

Hochschild, Arlie Russell. 2018. *Strangers in Their Own Land: Anger and Mourning on the American Right*. New York: The New Press.

Hoekstra, Erin, and Joseph Gerteis. 2019. "The Civic Side of Diversity: Ambivalence and Belonging at the Neighborhood Level." *City and Community* 18 (1): 195–212.

Holley, Emmajean. 2019. "Amid Revitalization Efforts, Residents Ponder What White River Junction's Identity Will Be." *Valley News*, July 10.

Jaworsky, Bernadette Nadya, Peggy Levitt, Wendy Cadge, Jessica Hejtmanek, and Sara R. Curran. 2012. "New Perspectives on Immigrant Contexts of Reception: The Cultural Armature of Cities." *Nordic Journal of Migration Research* 2 (1): 78–88.

Johnson, Kenneth M. 2022. *Rural America Lost Population over the Past Decade for the First Time in History*. Durham, NH: University of New Hampshire, Carsey School of Public Policy.

Keating, Joshua. 2020. "The Real Reason Why Republicans Keep Saying 'We're a Republic, Not a Democracy.'" *Slate*, October 13.

Keene, Danya E., and Mark B. Padilla. 2014. "Spatial Stigma and Health Inequality." *Critical Public Health* 24 (4): 392–404.

Kendi, Ibram X. 2020. "We're Still Living and Dying in the Slaveholders' Republic." *The Atlantic*, May 4. https://www.theatlantic.com/ideas/archive/2020/05/what-freedom-means-trump/611083/.

Kenyon, Jim. 2016. "People First in Claremont." *Valley News*, July 16.

Kenyon, Jim. 2022. "Fireworks as Flags Fly in Hartford." *Valley News*, June 25.

Keohane, Joe. 2018. "Beauty Is in the Eye of the Beholder: An Expat's Love Letter to New England." *Boston Magazine*, January 23.

Kunkel, Kathy. 2016. "Tamaqua Residents More Optimistic, Survey Finds." *Times News*, June 28.

Kwate, Naa Oyo A., and Ilan H. Meyer. 2011. "On Sticks and Stones and Broken Bones: Stereotypes and African American Health." *Du Bois Review* 8 (1): 191–198.

Kymlicka, Will. 1995. *Multicultural Citizenship: A Liberal Theory of Minority Rights*. Oxford Political Theory. Oxford: Oxford University Press.

Lamont, Michèle. 2018. "Addressing Recognition Gaps: Destigmatization and the Reduction of Inequality." *American Sociological Review* 83 (3): 419–444.

Lamont, Michèle. 2023. *Seeing Others: How Recognition Works and How It Can Heal a Divided World*. New York: One Signal Publishers.

Lamont, Michèle, and Sada Aksartova. 2002. "Ordinary Cosmopolitanisms: Strategies for Bridging Racial Boundaries among Working-Class Men." *Theory, Culture & Society* 19 (4): 1–25.

Lamont, Michèle, and Virág Molnár. 2002. "The Study of Boundaries Across the Social Sciences." *Annual Review of Sociology* 28: 167–195.

Lichter, Daniel T. 2012. "Immigration and the New Racial Diversity in Rural America." *Rural Sociology* 77 (1): 3–35.

Lichter, Daniel T., and David L. Brown. 2011. "Rural America in an Urban Society: Changing Spatial and Social Boundaries." *Annual Review of Sociology* 37: 565–592.

Lichter, Daniel T., and Kenneth M. Johnson. 2023. "Urbanization and the Paradox of Rural Population Decline: Racial and Regional Variation." *Socius: Sociological Research for a Dynamic World* 9: 1–21.

Lichter, Daniel T., Domenico Parisi, and Michael C. Taquino. 2018. "White Integration or Segregation? The Racial and Ethnic Transformation of Rural and Small Town America." *City and Community* 17 (3): 702–719.

Lindsey, Alex, Eden King, Michelle Hebl, and Noah Levine. 2015. "The Impact of Method, Motivation, and Empathy on Diversity Training Effectiveness." *Journal of Business and Psychology* 30: 605–617.

Lung-Amam, Willow S. 2017. *Trespassers? Asian Americans and the Battle for Suburbia*. Oakland: University of California Press.

Martineau, Wendy. 2012. "Misrecognition and Cross-Cultural Understanding: Shaping the Space for a 'Fusion of Horizons.'" *Ethnicities* 12 (2): 161–177.

McDermott, Jessica, and Tyler Work. 2019. *Affordable Housing in the Upper Valley*. Hanover, NH: The Nelson A. Rockefeller Center at Dartmouth College.

McDermott, Monica, and Annie Ferguson. 2022. "Sociology of Whiteness." *Annual Review of Sociology* 48: 257–276.

McEwen, Bruce S. 1998. "Stress, Adaptation, and Disease: Allostasis and Allostatic Load." *Annals of the New York Academy of Sciences* 840 (1): 33–44.

Meghji, Ali. 2018. "Activating Controlling Images in the Racialized Interaction Order: Black Middle-Class Interactions and the Creativity of Racist Action." *Symbolic Interaction* 42 (2): 229–249.

Merriman, Anna. 2020. "Scott Decries Targeting of Family from New York in Hartford." *Valley News*, May 13.

Mueller, Jennifer C. 2020. "Racial Ideology or Racial Ignorance? An Alternative Theory of Racial Cognition." *Sociological Theory* 38 (2): 142–169.

Neal, Sarah, Katy Bennett, Allan Cochrane, and Giles Mohan. 2013. "Living Multiculture: Understanding the New Spatial and Social Relations of Ethnicity and Multiculture in England." *Environment and Planning C: Politics and Space* 31 (2): 308–323.

Nelson, Mia. 2020. "'We Are Acknowledging They Are Here': Migrant Farmworkers in the Upper Valley and Dartmouth FUERZA." *Dartmouth Sustainability*, October 15.

Nelson, Peter B., and Wright Frost. 2022. "Migration Responses to the COVID-19 Pandemic: A Case Study of New England Showing Movements down the Urban Hierarchy and Ensuing Impacts on Real Estate Markets." *The Professional Geographer* 75 (3): 415–429.

Ngai, Mae M. 2004. "From Colonial Subject to Undesirable Alien: Filipino Migration in the Invisible Empire." In *Impossible Subjects: Illegal Aliens and the Making of Modern America*, 96–126. Princeton: Princeton University Press.

O'Connor, Kevin. 2021. "Stratton Town Report Cover Draws Attention for All the Wrong Reasons." *VT Digger*, February 24.

O'Grady, Patrick. 2022. "Claremont Businesses Upbeat as Pleasant Street Renovations Wind Down." *Valley News*, August 11.

Okamoto, Dina, and Kim Ebert. 2016. "Group Boundaries, Immigrant Inclusion, and the Politics of Immigrant-Native Relations." *American Behavioral Scientist* 60 (2): 224–250.

Pape, Robert A. 2022. *American Face of Insurrection: Analysis of Individuals Charged for Storming the US Capitol on January 6, 2021*. Chicago Project on Security and Threats, January 5.

Parekh, Bhikhu. 2005. *Unity and Diversity in Multicultural Societies*. Geneva: International Institute for Labour Studies.

Perrin, Noel. 1980. "The Rural Immigration Law." In *Second Person Rural: More Essays of a Sometime Farmer*. Boston: David R. Godine.

Pierson, George Wilson. 1955. "The Obstinate Concept of New England: A Study in Denudation." *The New England Quarterly* 28 (1): 3–17.

Pilgeram, Ryanne. 2021. *Pushed Out: Contested Development and Rural Gentrification in the US West*. Seattle: University of Washington Press.

Post, Chris W., and Mark A. Rhodes II. 2022. "Decolonizing Memory Work? Textual Politics of Settler State Historical Markers Engaging Indigenous Peoples in Kansas." *ACME: An International Journal for Critical Geographies* 21 (5): 540–559.

Ragsdale, Kathie. 2018. "The Upper Valley's Economic Upper Hand." *Business NH Magazine*, February 14.

Rauner Special Collections Library. 2015. "Owners of the Green." https://raunerlibrary.blogspot.com/2015/06/owners-of-green.html.

Rogers, Josh. 2022. "N.H. House Rejects Measure Banning the Use of Native American Symbols as Mascots." New Hampshire Public Radio, March 16.

Sacchetti, Maria. 2022. "A Rural County in Iowa That Supported Trump Turns to Latinos to Grow." *The Washington Post*, May 14.

Schafft, Kai A. 2018. "Busted Amidst the Boom: The Creation of New Insecurities and Inequalities Within Pennsylvania's Shale Gas Boomtowns." *Rural Sociology* 83 (3): 503–531.

Schwarzwalder, Rob. 2014. "Conservatives and the Constitution." *Public Discourse*, January 24.

Seaton, Jaimie. 2017. "New Hampshire Hanging: Parents of Accused Teen Say It Was an Accident Not a Lynching." *Newsweek*, September 23.

Sherman, Jennifer. 2006. "Coping with Rural Poverty: Economic Survival and Moral Capital in Rural America." *Social Forces* 85 (2): 891–913.

Sherman, Jennifer. 2018. "'Not Allowed to Inherit My Kingdom': Amenity Development and Social Inequality in the Rural West." *Rural Sociology* 83 (1): 174–207.

Simmel, Georg. 1908. "The Stranger." In *Excurs über den Fremden*, 509–512. Leipzig: Duncker and Humblot.

Small, Mario Luis. 2009. "'How Many Cases Do I Need?' On Science and the Logic of Case Selection in Field-Based Research." *Ethnography* 10 (1): 5–38.

Sohoni, Deenesh, and Tracy W. Sohoni. 2014. "Perceptions of Immigrant Criminality: Crime and Social Boundaries." *The Sociological Quarterly* 55 (1): 49–71.

Sonke, Jill, Tasha Golden, Samantha Francois, Jamie Hand, Anita Chandra, Lydia Clemmons, David Fakunle, Maria Rosario Jackson, Susan Magsamen, Victor Rubin, Kelly Sams, and Stacey Springs. 2019. *Creating Healthy Communities Through Cross-Sector Collaboration* (white paper). ArtPlace America. Gainesville: University of Florida Center for Arts in Medicine.

Stewart-Bouley, Shay. 2022. "I Have a Confession." *Black Girl in Maine* (blog), December 23. https://blackgirlinmaine.com/activism/i-have-a-confession/.

Taylor, Charles. 1994. "The Politics of Recognition." In *Multiculturalism: Examining the Politics of Recognition*, edited by Amy Gutmann, 25–73. Princeton: Princeton University Press.

TEDx Talks. 2011. "Jay Smooth—How I Learned to Stop Worrying and Love Discussing Race."

Timmermans, Stefan, and Iddo Tavory. 2012. "The Construction in Qualitative Research: From Grounded Theory to Abductive Analysis." *Sociological Theory* 30 (3): 167–186.

Town of Hartford. 2024. "Our History." https://hartford-vt.org/2543/Our-History.

Tree, Christina. 2014. "The 'Upper Valley': A Place of 'Unexpected Discoveries.'" *Yankee Magazine*, August 4.

Tuan, Yi-Fu. 1980. "Rootedness versus Sense of Place." *Landscape* 24: 3–8.

Tucker, Aviezer. 1994. "In Search of Home." *Journal of Applied Philosophy* 11 (2): 181–187.

Valley News. 2019. "NH AG: Evidence Didn't Support Hate Crime Charge in Claremont Near-Hanging." *VT Digger*, August 7.

Walton, Emily. 2024. Humans of the Upper Valley. https://sites.dartmouth.edu/humansoftheuppervalley/.

Weiss-Tisman, Howard. 2020. "Governor Condemns Xenophobia, Racism Following Hartford Incident." *Vermont Public*, May 13. https://www.vermontpublic.org/vpr-news/2020-05-13/governor-condemns-xenophobia-racism-following-hartford-incident.

Wikipedia. 2024. "The Green (Dartmouth College)." https://en.wikipedia.org/wiki/The_Green_(Dartmouth_College).

Williams, David R. 2018. "Stress and the Mental Health of Populations of Color: Advancing Our Understanding of Race-Related Stressors." *Journal of Health and Social Behavior* 59 (4): 466–485.

Williams, Monnica T., Angela M. Haeny, and Samantha C. Holmes. 2021. "Post-traumatic Stress Disorder and Racial Trauma." *PTSD Research Quarterly* 32 (1): 1–9.

Wingfield, Adia Harvey. 2010. "Are Some Emotions Marked "Whites Only"? Racialized Feeling Rules in Professional Workplaces." *Social Problems* 57 (2): 251–268.

Yin, Robert K. 2009. *Case Study Research: Design and Methods*. Applied Social Research Methods Series, vol. 5, edited by Leonard Bickman and Debra J. Rog. Los Angeles: Sage.

Index

Afghan refugees, 116

African Americans, 77, 78, 81, 103, 124; in Claremont, NH, 26–27t; in Hanover, NH, 30–31t; in Hartford, VT, 34–35t; Nigerian, 43, 87, 99, 107; sociodemographic characteristics, 125t. *See also* Black people

Afro-Latinas, 15, 43, 85

amenity migration, 6, 129

America. *See* United States

American Rescue Plan Act, 114–115

Anderson, Elijah, 77

anti-racism, 120–121, 136n5

anxiety, 57, 93; anticipatory, 58; status, 24; as symptom of homesickness, 93, 96–100

Arbery, Ahmaud, 62, 63

Asian Americans, 3, 21, 106, 124; Bengali, 100; Chinese, 15, 16, 17, 46, 65, 76, 93, 98, 110, 111, 123; in Clare-

mont, NH, 26–27t; Filipino, 1, 17, 68, 75, 95, 104; in Hanover, NH, 30–31t; in Hartford, VT, 34–35t; Indian, 4, 14, 41, 42, 46, 63, 70, 74, 85, 97; Indonesian, 16, 83, 99; Japanese, 82; Korean, 15, 42, 67, 96, 110, 123; Pakistani, 94; sociodemographic characteristics, 125t; South Asian, 68, 86, 97, 103; Vietnamese, 123

assimilation, 53, 73, 97, 115; culture of, 53–61

Baldwin, James, 95

behaviors, 88; behavioral expectations, 53, 54, 56, 58; cultural, 61; cultural characteristics guide, 37; for group membership, 76; normative, 59; public vs. private, 41; racist, 52; rudeness, 40; of white residents, 53–54

The authorized representative in the EU for product safety and compliance is:
Mare Nostrum Group
B.V Doelen 72
4831 GR Breda
The Netherlands

www.ingramcontent.com/pod-product-compliance
Lightning Source LLC
Jackson TN
JSHW020720090326
98924JS00008B/491